The Real Story of Apex

France's Fierce Entry Fragger – Unauthorized

Anjali Esposito

ISBN: 9781779698896
Imprint: Telephasic Workshop
Copyright © 2024 Anjali Esposito.
All Rights Reserved.

Contents

The Rise of Apex 13
Behind the Gamer Tag 24

Trials and Triumphs 45
Trials and Triumphs 45
The Intel Championship 48
The Epsilon Era 55
The Showdown with Rival Teams 65
A Legacy in the Making 72

Bibliography 75

Trials and Tribulations 81
Trials and Tribulations 81
The Betrayal 84
The Road to Redemption 90
The Struggle with Mental Health 98
Rising from the Ashes 105

The Legend Lives On 113
The Legend Lives On 113
Establishing a Legacy 115
Life Beyond Esports 119
The Final Chapter 126
Unauthorized, But Worth It 133

Bibliography 141

Index 143

The Early Years

In the grand tapestry of competitive gaming, every legend has a humble beginning, and so too does the tale of Anjali Esposito, known to the world as Apex. Born in the picturesque landscape of France, Anjali's early years were marked by a blend of curiosity and an insatiable thirst for adventure. From the moment she could grasp a controller, she was captivated by the digital realms that beckoned her from the screen.

A Passion for Gaming

Anjali's journey into the world of gaming began at the tender age of six, when her father gifted her a modest gaming console. This simple act ignited a spark that would grow into a blazing passion. The allure of pixelated worlds and the thrill of virtual conquests became an integral part of her childhood. As she navigated through various titles, from platformers to RPGs, she began to understand the mechanics of gameplay, developing a keen eye for strategy and an instinct for competition.

Discovering Competitive Esports

As the years rolled on, Anjali discovered the burgeoning world of esports. It was a revelation that transformed her perception of gaming from a solitary pastime to a vibrant, competitive arena. She immersed herself in online forums and watched streams of professional players, absorbing their techniques and strategies. The competitive spirit that had been kindled in her youth began to flourish, leading her to join local tournaments where she could test her skills against others.

Facing Challenges and Criticism

However, the path to becoming a professional esports athlete was not without its trials. Anjali faced skepticism from peers and critics alike, who often dismissed gaming as a frivolous pursuit. The societal stigma surrounding gaming posed significant challenges, as she battled to prove that her passion was not merely a hobby but a legitimate career path.

Building a Supportive Network

In the face of adversity, Anjali sought solace and strength in a supportive network of friends and family. Her parents, initially hesitant about her gaming ambitions, gradually became her staunchest allies, attending tournaments and cheering her on. Additionally, she connected with like-minded individuals through online communities, where she found encouragement and camaraderie. This network would prove invaluable as she navigated the tumultuous waters of competitive gaming.

The Road to Becoming a Pro

With a foundation built on passion and support, Anjali began to hone her skills with relentless determination. She dedicated countless hours to practice, analyzing gameplay footage and refining her strategies. The road to becoming a professional was fraught with challenges, but each setback only fueled her desire to succeed.

Through perseverance, she earned her place in the competitive scene, participating in increasingly prestigious tournaments. The thrill of competition, the adrenaline rush of clutch plays, and the camaraderie of team dynamics became her new reality. Anjali was no longer just a gamer; she was on the precipice of becoming Apex, a name that would soon resonate in the annals of esports history.

In conclusion, the early years of Anjali Esposito were characterized by a passionate pursuit of gaming, a discovery of competitive esports, and the resilience to overcome societal challenges. These formative experiences laid the groundwork for her future as a top-tier entry fragger, setting the stage for a legendary career that would inspire countless others in the gaming community.

$$E = mc^2 \qquad (1)$$

Where E represents energy, m is mass, and c is the speed of light in a vacuum, illustrating the foundational principle of transformation that mirrors Anjali's evolution from a casual gamer to a competitive force in esports.

As we delve deeper into Anjali's story, we will explore the rise of Apex and the trials and triumphs that shaped her journey into the realm of professional gaming.

The Early Years

The genesis of any esports athlete is often a tale woven with threads of passion, perseverance, and the occasional pitfall. Anjali Esposito's journey into the vibrant world of competitive gaming began in the quaint suburbs of Lyon, France. Born into a family that valued creativity and exploration, Anjali's early years were marked by an insatiable curiosity and a penchant for adventure. The young Anjali was not just another child; she was an explorer in her own right, navigating the uncharted territories of digital realms.

A Passion for Gaming

From the tender age of six, Anjali found herself captivated by the flickering lights of her family's old computer. The allure of pixelated worlds and the thrill of virtual conquests ignited a passion that would shape her future. Her first encounter with gaming came in the form of a simple platformer, where she would spend countless hours jumping, running, and collecting coins. This early experience laid the groundwork for her burgeoning interest in more complex games, eventually leading her to the realm of first-person shooters (FPS).

As she transitioned from casual gaming to more competitive titles, Anjali's natural talent began to shine. She was not merely playing for fun; she was honing her skills, developing reflexes that would later define her career. The adrenaline rush of outmaneuvering opponents and achieving victory became a powerful motivator. However, as with any journey, the path was not without its challenges.

Discovering Competitive Esports

The real turning point in Anjali's life came when she stumbled upon a local gaming tournament at the age of thirteen. It was a vibrant gathering of gamers, showcasing skill and camaraderie, and it was here that she first tasted the thrill of competitive play. The atmosphere was electric, filled with the sounds of keyboard clacks and enthusiastic cheers. Anjali knew at that moment that she wanted to be part of this world.

Her participation in the tournament was both exhilarating and eye-opening. Although she did not win, the experience ignited a fire within her. She realized that competitive gaming was not just about individual skill; it was about strategy, teamwork, and the relentless pursuit of excellence. This revelation would become a cornerstone of her approach to esports.

Facing Challenges and Criticism

However, the road to becoming a professional esports athlete was fraught with obstacles. Anjali faced skepticism from peers and family alike. Many viewed gaming as a mere pastime, a distraction from academics and real-life responsibilities. Critics often questioned her commitment and dedication, casting doubt on her aspirations. Yet, rather than succumbing to the negativity, Anjali used it as fuel for her determination.

She began to immerse herself in the gaming community, seeking out mentors and fellow enthusiasts who shared her passion. Through online forums and local meetups, she connected with other gamers who understood the challenges she faced.

This supportive network became invaluable, providing encouragement and guidance as she navigated the complexities of competitive gaming.

Building a Supportive Network

Anjali's journey was not a solitary one. She quickly learned the importance of surrounding herself with like-minded individuals who believed in her potential. This network included seasoned players who offered insights into gameplay strategies, as well as friends who provided emotional support during tough times. Together, they formed a tight-knit community that celebrated victories and learned from defeats.

In addition to her peers, Anjali sought inspiration from established esports athletes. She studied their gameplay, analyzed their strategies, and absorbed their philosophies. This dedication to learning became a hallmark of her character, setting her apart from many aspiring gamers. Anjali understood that to succeed, she needed to be both a student and a competitor.

The Road to Becoming a Pro

With each passing year, Anjali's skills sharpened, and her passion for gaming deepened. She dedicated herself to rigorous practice, often spending hours perfecting her aim and mastering game mechanics. Her commitment paid off as she began to participate in more competitive tournaments, steadily climbing the ranks and earning recognition within the community.

The transition from amateur to professional was a gradual one, marked by countless hours of practice and a relentless pursuit of improvement. Anjali faced setbacks, including losses that tested her resolve. However, with each challenge, she grew stronger, more determined to prove herself in a world dominated by fierce competition.

As she approached her late teens, Anjali Esposito was no longer just a passionate gamer; she was on the brink of becoming a professional esports athlete. The stage was set for her to make her mark in the industry, and the world was about to witness the rise of Apex, France's fierce entry fragger.

Discovering Competitive Esports

The journey into the realm of competitive esports is akin to stepping into an enchanted arena where skill meets strategy, and passion transforms into performance. For Anjali Esposito, known in the gaming world as Apex, this journey began with a spark of curiosity that ignited a fervor for competition.

In the early days, Apex found himself drawn to the vibrant community of gamers who shared his enthusiasm for digital battles. It was during this formative period that he encountered his first competitive tournament, a local LAN event that would serve as a pivotal moment in his burgeoning career. The atmosphere was electric, filled with the sounds of clattering keyboards, the murmurs of strategy, and the palpable tension of rivalry.

$$\text{Skill Level} = \frac{\text{Practice Hours} \times \text{Game Knowledge}}{\text{Distractions}} \quad (2)$$

This equation highlights a fundamental principle in esports: skill is not merely a product of innate talent but is significantly influenced by the amount of practice and knowledge one accumulates. Apex quickly realized that to excel, he would need to immerse himself in the intricacies of the game, dedicating countless hours to honing his skills while minimizing distractions.

As he began to participate in more tournaments, the challenges became increasingly pronounced. The competitive landscape was rife with seasoned players who had already established their reputations. Apex faced formidable opponents, each with their own unique playstyles and strategies. The pressure to perform was intense, and the fear of failure loomed large.

$$\text{Pressure} = \text{Expectations} - \text{Preparation} \quad (3)$$

This equation encapsulates the psychological struggle that many athletes face. In Apex's case, the expectations from fans, peers, and even himself weighed heavily on his shoulders. However, he understood that preparation was the antidote to pressure. He began to study his opponents meticulously, analyzing their gameplay to identify weaknesses and opportunities for exploitation.

Despite the hurdles, Apex found solace in the camaraderie of his fellow gamers. The supportive network he built became a cornerstone of his journey. These connections provided not only friendship but also a wealth of knowledge and experience. They shared strategies, offered constructive criticism, and celebrated each other's successes. This environment of mutual support was crucial in fostering resilience and determination.

Apex's breakthrough moment came during a regional tournament where he showcased his signature entry fragging style. This aggressive playstyle, characterized by quick decision-making and precise aiming, set him apart from his peers. He understood that entry fraggers play a pivotal role in team dynamics, often setting the pace of engagements and creating opportunities for their teammates.

$$\text{Team Success} = \text{Entry Fragger Impact} + \text{Team Coordination} \quad (4)$$

This equation illustrates the symbiotic relationship between an entry fragger and the team. Apex's ability to secure early kills not only boosted his confidence but also galvanized his teammates, creating a ripple effect of morale and momentum. His performance did not go unnoticed; he began to gain recognition within the esports community, earning invitations to more prestigious events.

However, the path to success was not without its obstacles. Apex faced criticism from some corners of the community, questioning his aggressive style and decision-making. Yet, rather than succumb to doubt, he embraced these critiques as opportunities for growth. He sought feedback from experienced players and coaches, continually refining his approach and expanding his understanding of the game.

The discovery of competitive esports was not merely about the thrill of competition; it was a transformative experience that shaped Apex into the player he would become. It taught him the importance of resilience, the value of teamwork, and the necessity of constant self-improvement.

In retrospect, the journey from a casual gamer to a competitive entry fragger was marked by trials and triumphs, each contributing to the tapestry of his career. As Apex continued to navigate the ever-evolving landscape of esports, he remained committed to his passion, driven by the desire to leave a lasting impact on the gaming world.

In summary, discovering competitive esports was a multifaceted experience for Apex. It involved not only the thrill of competition but also the cultivation of skills, the forging of relationships, and the overcoming of challenges. This chapter of his life laid the foundation for the legendary career that was yet to unfold.

Facing Challenges and Criticism

In the tumultuous world of esports, where the stakes are as high as the adrenaline rush that comes with competition, Anjali Esposito, known to her legion of fans as Apex, faced her fair share of challenges and criticism. The journey from a passionate gamer to a recognized professional was fraught with obstacles that tested her resolve, skill, and mental fortitude.

The Weight of Expectations

As Apex began to carve her niche in the esports arena, the expectations from fans, sponsors, and her team mounted. The pressure to perform at peak levels during competitions is not merely a matter of personal ambition; it is a complex interplay of psychological factors that can significantly impact an athlete's performance. According to the *Yerkes-Dodson Law*, there exists an optimal level of arousal for peak performance, where too little arousal can lead to underperformance, while too much can result in anxiety and detrimental effects on gameplay.

$$\text{Performance} = f(\text{Arousal}) \tag{5}$$

In Apex's case, the initial excitement of competition soon morphed into a daunting pressure that threatened to overwhelm her. Critics were quick to scrutinize her every move, often attributing her failures to a lack of talent rather than acknowledging the inherent difficulties of competing at such high levels. This criticism, while sometimes constructive, often veered into the realm of personal attacks, leading to a detrimental impact on her mental health.

Dealing with Online Harassment

The digital landscape of esports is notorious for its harsh realities, particularly the prevalence of online harassment. Social media platforms, while serving as a means of connection, also became a breeding ground for negativity. Apex found herself the target of trolls and detractors who thrived on demeaning her abilities and questioning her place in the competitive scene.

The psychological toll of such harassment cannot be understated. Research indicates that exposure to negative comments can lead to increased anxiety, depression, and a diminished sense of self-worth. Apex, like many athletes, had to navigate this treacherous terrain, developing coping strategies to mitigate the effects of online hostility.

Building Resilience

In the face of adversity, resilience emerged as a critical trait for Apex. Resilience, defined as the ability to bounce back from setbacks, is essential in the high-pressure world of esports. A study conducted by *Smith et al. (2017)* highlights that resilient athletes are more likely to maintain focus and composure under pressure, leading to improved performance outcomes.

Apex sought support from her peers and mentors, recognizing that building a strong support network was paramount. Engaging with fellow gamers who had faced similar challenges provided her with valuable insights and strategies. This communal aspect of resilience not only fostered a sense of belonging but also reinforced her determination to succeed.

Learning from Criticism

Instead of allowing criticism to deter her, Apex began to view it as an opportunity for growth. Constructive criticism, when delivered appropriately, can serve as a catalyst for improvement. By analyzing feedback from coaches and experienced players, she was able to identify areas for enhancement in her gameplay.

For instance, during a pivotal tournament, Apex's decision-making under pressure was called into question. Rather than retreating into self-doubt, she embraced the feedback, dedicating herself to refining her strategic approach. This mindset shift exemplified the importance of adaptability in esports, where the meta can change rapidly, and players must evolve to remain competitive.

The Journey of Self-Discovery

Ultimately, facing challenges and criticism became a journey of self-discovery for Apex. She learned to embrace her identity as a gamer, recognizing that her worth was not solely defined by her performance in tournaments but also by her passion for gaming and her ability to inspire others. This realization was pivotal in transforming her relationship with competition, allowing her to enjoy the game for what it was—a thrilling and immersive experience.

In conclusion, the road to becoming a top-tier esports athlete is laden with challenges and criticism. For Apex, the ability to confront these obstacles head-on, coupled with a resilient mindset and a supportive network, paved the way for her eventual success. By embracing both the highs and lows of her journey, she not only solidified her place in the esports community but also emerged as a beacon of inspiration for aspiring gamers worldwide.

Building a Supportive Network

In the high-octane world of esports, where the stakes are as high as the adrenaline, building a supportive network is akin to constructing a fortress against the tempest of challenges that an athlete may face. For Anjali Esposito, better known by her gamer tag, Apex, this network became the bedrock upon which her illustrious career was built.

The Importance of a Supportive Network

A supportive network serves multiple purposes in the life of an esports athlete. It provides emotional support, practical advice, and often, a sense of belonging. The dynamics of such a network can be analyzed through the lens of social capital theory, which posits that social networks have value and can lead to tangible benefits. According to Bourdieu's theory of social capital, the resources available to an individual through their social networks can significantly influence their success [?].

In Apex's case, her network included family, friends, fellow gamers, and mentors who not only celebrated her victories but also helped her navigate the inevitable pitfalls of competitive gaming. For instance, during moments of self-doubt or criticism, her friends would rally around her, providing encouragement and reminding her of her capabilities. This emotional scaffolding was crucial, especially when facing the daunting pressures of high-stakes tournaments.

Overcoming Challenges

The journey to building a supportive network is fraught with challenges. Apex faced criticism early in her career, often from those who doubted her abilities in a male-dominated field. Such skepticism can lead to isolation, a phenomenon described by the "imposter syndrome," where individuals feel like frauds despite their accomplishments [?].

To combat this, Apex actively sought out communities where she felt valued. Online platforms like Discord and Twitch became sanctuaries where she could connect with like-minded individuals. These platforms facilitated interactions that were not only supportive but also educational. She learned from others' experiences and shared her own, creating a reciprocal relationship that enriched her understanding of the game and the esports landscape.

Building Relationships with Mentors

Mentorship played a pivotal role in Apex's journey. Finding mentors who understood the intricacies of the esports ecosystem allowed her to gain insights that were otherwise inaccessible. According to a study by Allen et al. (2004), mentorship relationships can significantly enhance career development and personal growth [?].

Apex connected with seasoned players and coaches who provided guidance on gameplay strategies and mental resilience. One notable mentor, a former champion known for his tactical acumen, helped her refine her signature playstyle. This relationship exemplified the power of mentorship in overcoming barriers and accelerating success.

The Role of Community Engagement

Engaging with the broader esports community also contributed to Apex's network. By participating in local tournaments and gaming events, she fostered connections with other players and fans. This engagement not only expanded her network but also increased her visibility within the esports scene.

For instance, after a particularly successful run at a regional tournament, Apex took the time to interact with fans and aspiring gamers. This act of community engagement created a positive feedback loop; as she inspired others, she also received encouragement in return, reinforcing her commitment to the sport.

The Balance of Personal and Professional Relationships

While building a supportive network is vital, it is equally important to maintain a balance between personal and professional relationships. Apex learned that while her gaming life was intensely competitive, her personal relationships provided the grounding necessary to cope with stress.

The equation for maintaining this balance can be expressed as:

$$B = \frac{P + C}{R}$$

Where:

- B = Balance
- P = Personal relationships
- C = Competitive relationships
- R = Responsibilities

Apex found that by nurturing her personal relationships, she could recharge and return to the competitive arena with renewed vigor. This balance proved essential during times of intense competition, where the pressure to perform could easily overshadow personal well-being.

Conclusion

In conclusion, building a supportive network is an essential aspect of an esports athlete's journey. For Apex, this network provided the emotional and practical support necessary to navigate the complexities of her career. By leveraging social capital, engaging with mentors, participating in community events, and maintaining a balance between personal and professional relationships, she forged a path to success that not only propelled her to the top of the esports world but also inspired a new generation of gamers. As she continues to evolve as a player and a person, the network she built remains a testament to the power of connection in the pursuit of greatness.

The Road to Becoming a Pro

In the world of esports, the journey from a casual gamer to a professional athlete is often fraught with challenges, sacrifices, and moments of self-discovery. For Anjali Esposito, known in the gaming community as Apex, this path was no different. The transition into professional gaming is not merely a leap into the spotlight; it requires a meticulous blend of skill, strategy, and mental fortitude.

Understanding the Landscape

The first step on the road to becoming a professional esports athlete is to understand the competitive landscape. This involves familiarizing oneself with the various games, the community dynamics, and the intricate web of teams and tournaments. Apex began by immersing herself in the competitive scene of her chosen game, studying the top players, their strategies, and the evolving meta.

The meta, or the most effective tactics available, is crucial for any aspiring pro. As the game evolves, so too must the players. Apex spent countless hours analyzing gameplay footage, dissecting strategies, and practicing relentlessly to adapt to the shifting tides of competition.

Skill Development

Skill development is paramount in the journey to professional gaming. Apex dedicated herself to honing her reflexes, aiming precision, and game sense—an innate understanding of the game's mechanics and flow. This required a rigorous training regimen, often involving:

- **Aim Training:** Utilizing software like Aim Lab or Kovaak's FPS Aim Trainer, she focused on improving her shooting accuracy and reaction times.
- **Game Mechanics:** Mastering the intricacies of her character and the game environment was essential. Apex practiced various movement techniques, weapon handling, and map navigation to gain an edge over her opponents.

- **Team Play:** Understanding that esports is a team sport, she engaged in scrims (practice matches) with local teams, learning to communicate effectively and develop synergy with her teammates.

Facing Challenges and Criticism

As with any ambitious journey, the road to professionalism is littered with obstacles. Apex encountered her fair share of challenges, including criticism from peers and the community. The pressure to perform and the fear of failure can be overwhelming. To combat this, she adopted a growth mindset, viewing criticism as an opportunity for improvement rather than a personal attack.

This mindset is supported by the work of psychologist Carol Dweck, who posits that individuals who embrace challenges and learn from criticism are more likely to achieve success. Apex learned to filter negative feedback and channel it into her training, thus transforming potential setbacks into stepping stones.

Building a Supportive Network

No journey is undertaken alone, and for Apex, building a supportive network was crucial. She sought mentors within the esports community—experienced players and coaches who could provide guidance and insight. Networking with fellow gamers allowed her to exchange strategies, receive feedback, and foster a sense of camaraderie.

Moreover, social media platforms, particularly Twitch and Discord, played a significant role in connecting with other gamers. Apex often participated in online discussions, shared her gameplay, and engaged with fans, all while cultivating a community that supported her ambitions.

The Road to Professionalism

The final stretch of the road to becoming a pro involved participating in amateur tournaments. Apex entered local competitions, often facing off against seasoned players. These experiences were invaluable, providing her with a taste of the competitive atmosphere and the pressure of high-stakes matches.

$$\text{Performance} = \text{Skill} + \text{Strategy} + \text{Mental Fortitude} \qquad (6)$$

This equation encapsulates the essence of competitive gaming. Apex realized that while skill and strategy are critical, mental fortitude—the ability to remain composed under pressure—often separates the good from the great.

Her dedication paid off when she caught the attention of a prominent esports organization, leading to her first official contract. This moment marked a significant milestone in her career, validating her hard work and determination.

Conclusion

The road to becoming a professional esports athlete is a complex journey filled with trials, tribulations, and triumphs. For Apex, each challenge was an opportunity for growth, and each victory was a testament to her relentless pursuit of excellence. As she stepped into the world of professional gaming, she carried with her the lessons learned along the way—lessons that would shape not only her career but also her identity as a fierce competitor in the esports arena.

The Rise of Apex

Joining a Prominent Team

In the world of esports, the transition from a hopeful contender to a recognized professional can often feel like traversing a labyrinthine path, fraught with challenges, triumphs, and the occasional twist of fate. For Anjali Esposito, known in the gaming realm as Apex, this journey took a decisive turn when she joined a prominent team, a moment that would not only define her career but also reshape the landscape of competitive gaming.

Apex's ascent began in the bustling streets of Paris, where the vibrant gaming community served as a backdrop for her burgeoning talent. After years of honing her skills in local tournaments and online leagues, the whispers of her prowess reached the ears of talent scouts from one of Europe's leading esports organizations, Team Valor. Known for their strategic gameplay and a roster of elite players, Team Valor was the dream team for any aspiring esports athlete.

The offer to join Team Valor came as a whirlwind, a mix of excitement and trepidation. The team had a reputation for not only winning but also for fostering a culture of excellence and innovation. Apex knew that this was her chance to step into the spotlight, but it also meant facing the daunting pressure that comes with being part of a high-caliber team.

$$\text{Team Success} = \text{Individual Skill} \times \text{Team Dynamics} \tag{7}$$

This equation encapsulates the essence of what Apex was about to experience. While her individual skill was undeniable, the success of Team Valor hinged on how well she could integrate into their existing dynamics.

Upon joining, Apex was immediately immersed in a rigorous training regimen. The team's coach, a seasoned veteran of the esports scene, emphasized the importance of synergy and communication. They implemented daily scrims, where strategies were tested and refined in real-time. Apex quickly learned that the chemistry between players could make or break a match.

$$\text{Synergy} = \sum_{i=1}^{n} \text{Player}_i^{\text{Skill}} \times \text{Communication}_{i,j} \tag{8}$$

In this equation, the synergy was quantified not just by individual skill but also by the communication between players. Apex found herself in a whirlwind of strategies, callouts, and tactical discussions that stretched her understanding of the game.

Yet, the transition was not without its challenges. Apex faced skepticism from some veteran players who questioned her ability to adapt to the team's high standards. The weight of their expectations felt like a double-edged sword; it drove her to push her limits but also cast shadows of doubt in her mind.

To combat these challenges, Apex leaned into her supportive network, a close-knit group of friends and fellow gamers who had been with her since the early days. They reminded her of the passion that fueled her journey and the countless hours spent perfecting her craft. With their encouragement, she began to thrive within Team Valor, developing a signature playstyle that combined aggressive entry fragging with an uncanny ability to read the opponent's movements.

As the months rolled on, Apex's contributions became undeniable. Her exceptional skills in securing early picks transformed the team's approach to engagements, allowing them to dictate the pace of the game. The synergy within Team Valor began to flourish, and the fruits of their labor became evident as they started racking up victories in regional tournaments.

The moment of breakthrough came during the European Championship, where Team Valor faced off against their fiercest rivals. Apex, with her newfound confidence, delivered a performance that would be etched in the annals of esports history. Her aggressive plays and clutch moments led Team Valor to a stunning victory, solidifying her status as a top entry fragger.

The accolades and recognition that followed were not merely trophies; they were the validation of years of hard work and resilience. Apex had not only joined a prominent team but had also carved out her identity within it. The journey from a solitary gamer to a celebrated member of Team Valor was a testament to her dedication and passion for the craft.

In the months that followed, Apex would continue to evolve, not just as a player but as a cultural icon within the esports community. Her journey had just begun, and the world was eager to see what the fierce entry fragger from France would accomplish next.

$$\text{Legacy} = \text{Impact} + \text{Inspiration} \qquad (9)$$

As Apex settled into her role, she realized that her legacy would be defined not just by her victories but by her ability to inspire the next generation of gamers. Joining Team Valor was merely the first chapter in a story that promised to be filled with trials, triumphs, and a lasting impact on the world of esports.

Developing a Signature Playstyle

In the vibrant tapestry of competitive gaming, a player's signature playstyle serves as their unique fingerprint—an intricate blend of strategy, skill, and personal flair. For Anjali Esposito, known in the esports realm as Apex, the journey to cultivating this distinctive approach was not merely a path of trial and error; it was a calculated expedition through the labyrinth of competitive dynamics.

Understanding the Mechanics

At the heart of Apex's signature playstyle lies a profound understanding of game mechanics. To develop a playstyle that stands out, a player must first grasp the fundamental principles of the game. This includes knowledge of character abilities, map layouts, and the physics governing gameplay. For instance, in first-person shooters (FPS), the mechanics of movement—such as strafing, crouching, and jumping—play a pivotal role in evading enemy fire while maintaining accuracy.

The equation for optimal movement can be expressed as:

$$M = \frac{D}{T} \qquad (10)$$

where M represents movement efficiency, D is distance covered, and T is time taken. Apex's commitment to mastering this equation allowed him to navigate the battlefield with an agility that left opponents bewildered.

Crafting a Tactical Approach

Apex's tactical approach is characterized by his aggressive entry fragging, a role that demands not only precision shooting but also a keen awareness of team dynamics.

Entry fraggers are often the first to engage the enemy, tasked with creating openings for their teammates. This necessitates a blend of risk-taking and strategic foresight.

To illustrate, consider the scenario of a typical round in a competitive match. The entry fragger must evaluate the potential risks and rewards associated with pushing into enemy territory. The decision-making process can be modeled using a risk-reward framework:

$$R = P \times V - C \qquad (11)$$

where R is the overall reward, P is the probability of success, V is the value of the objective, and C is the cost of failure. Apex honed his ability to assess these variables in real-time, allowing him to make split-second decisions that often turned the tide of battle.

Adapting to Opponents

A crucial aspect of developing a signature playstyle is the ability to adapt to the ever-changing landscape of competitive gaming. Apex recognized that each opponent presents a unique challenge, necessitating a flexible approach. By studying rival teams and their strategies, he was able to anticipate their moves and counter them effectively.

For example, during a high-stakes tournament, Apex faced off against Team Pinnacle, known for their defensive playstyle. Instead of adhering strictly to his aggressive tactics, he adapted by employing a more cautious approach, utilizing the element of surprise to dismantle their defenses. This adaptability is encapsulated in the principle of situational awareness, which can be described by the following equation:

$$SA = \frac{I}{E} \qquad (12)$$

where SA represents situational awareness, I is the information available, and E is the environment's complexity. Apex's ability to enhance his situational awareness allowed him to thrive in chaotic scenarios, transforming potential pitfalls into opportunities for victory.

Incorporating Psychological Elements

Beyond mechanics and tactics, the psychological aspect of gaming cannot be overlooked. Apex understood that a signature playstyle is not solely about execution; it is also about instilling fear in opponents and inspiring confidence in teammates. The mental game can be quantified through the concept of pressure, which can be expressed as:

$$P = \frac{F}{A} \qquad (13)$$

where P represents pressure, F is the force of competition, and A is the area of influence. Apex's ability to apply psychological pressure often led to mistakes from his opponents, allowing him to capitalize on their errors.

The Evolution of Apex's Playstyle

As Apex continued to compete at higher levels, his playstyle evolved. He began to incorporate elements from various gaming genres, experimenting with unconventional strategies that caught opponents off guard. This evolution can be seen in his use of environmental awareness, leveraging the terrain to gain tactical advantages.

For instance, utilizing verticality in maps allowed him to surprise enemies from unexpected angles, transforming traditional strategies into innovative maneuvers. This adaptability not only solidified his reputation as a top fragger but also inspired a new generation of gamers to think outside the box.

Conclusion

In conclusion, the development of a signature playstyle is a multifaceted journey that encompasses mechanics, tactics, adaptability, and psychology. For Apex, this journey was marked by relentless practice, a willingness to learn, and an insatiable desire to push the boundaries of what is possible in esports. As he continues to carve his legacy, his signature playstyle remains a testament to the power of innovation and determination in the world of competitive gaming.

Early Tournament Successes

As the sun began to rise over the competitive esports landscape, Anjali Esposito, known to the world as Apex, was poised to make a name for himself in the thrilling arena of first-person shooters. The early tournaments became the crucible in which Apex would forge his identity as a formidable entry fragger, a title that would resonate through the annals of esports history.

The First Taste of Victory

Apex's journey into competitive gaming began with local tournaments, where the stakes were low but the passion was palpable. It was here that he first tasted victory, winning a small-scale event in Paris, which he later described as "a spark that ignited a wildfire." The adrenaline rush of competing against like-minded individuals, coupled with the thrill of victory, was intoxicating.

This initial success was not merely a stroke of luck; it was a demonstration of his innate talent and skill. The tournament format was a double-elimination bracket, where teams had to win two out of three matches to advance. Apex's team, known as "The Rising Stars," showcased a strategic playstyle that emphasized teamwork and communication, which was pivotal in their success.

Building Momentum

Following this victory, Apex and his team began to attract attention. They participated in more tournaments, each time refining their strategies and honing their skills. The experience gained from each match was invaluable, allowing Apex to develop a keen understanding of game mechanics and the psychology of his opponents.

One of the significant turning points came during the "Paris Clash," a regional tournament that boasted a modest prize pool but drew competitors from across France. Apex's team faced formidable opponents, yet they emerged victorious, showcasing a combination of aggressive tactics and calculated decision-making.

$$\text{Team Performance} = \frac{\text{Wins}}{\text{Total Matches}} \times 100\% \qquad (14)$$

Here, Apex's team recorded an impressive win rate of 75%, a statistic that would become a cornerstone of their reputation. This performance was not just about numbers; it was about the confidence that victory instilled in the players. Apex's ability to secure early kills and create openings for his teammates became a defining characteristic of his playstyle.

Recognition and Opportunities

With each tournament win, Apex garnered recognition not just from fans, but also from sponsors and established teams. This attention led to an invitation to participate in the "European Esports Championship," a prestigious event that served as a gateway to the international stage.

The championship was a grueling test of skill, featuring some of the best teams from across Europe. Apex's team, now known as "Apex Predators," faced a series of nail-biting matches. The pressure was palpable, yet Apex thrived in these high-stakes environments. His ability to maintain composure under pressure was a testament to his mental fortitude.

The Turning Point

A pivotal moment occurred during a match against "Team Vanguard," a well-respected squad with a history of dominating the European scene. Apex's performance in this match was nothing short of extraordinary. He secured a staggering 20 eliminations, leading his team to a decisive victory. This performance not only solidified his status as a top fragger but also caught the attention of talent scouts from major esports organizations.

The victory against Team Vanguard was a defining moment in Apex's career. It was not merely about winning; it was about proving to himself and the world that he belonged in the upper echelons of competitive gaming.

Setting the Stage for Greatness

The early tournament successes laid the foundation for Apex's burgeoning career. They provided him with the experience, recognition, and confidence necessary to take the next step. Each match was a lesson, each victory a building block towards greatness.

Apex's journey was not without its challenges; however, the early successes served as a reminder of what was possible. They ignited a fire within him, a relentless drive to push the boundaries of his capabilities.

As he prepared for the next chapter in his career, Apex understood that the road ahead would be fraught with challenges, but he was ready. The early tournaments were not just stepping stones; they were the very essence of his identity as a gamer. The stage was set for a meteoric rise, and Apex was determined to seize every opportunity that came his way.

$$\text{Future Success} = \text{Current Skill Level} + \text{Experience} + \text{Dedication} \quad (15)$$

In conclusion, the early tournament successes of Apex were not just victories on the scoreboard; they were milestones in a journey that would see him become a legend in the world of esports. With each match played, he was not just an athlete; he was an artist, crafting a legacy that would inspire generations to come.

Gaining Recognition on the International Stage

As the digital dust settled from the early skirmishes of Anjali Esposito's career, the world began to take notice of a player who was not merely a participant but a force to be reckoned with. The journey to international recognition is often paved with trials, tribulations, and a sprinkle of serendipity—elements that would shape Anjali's ascent in the competitive gaming arena.

The first significant breakthrough came during the **Global Esports Championship** (GEC) held in Paris, a city that holds a special place in the hearts of many gamers. It was here that Anjali, under the gamer tag "Apex," faced off against some of the best players from around the globe. The tournament format, a double-elimination bracket, meant that every match was a test of not just skill but also mental fortitude.

$$\text{Win Rate} = \frac{\text{Number of Wins}}{\text{Total Matches}} \tag{16}$$

In the GEC, Apex's win rate soared to an impressive 75%, a statistic that caught the attention of analysts and fans alike. This was not merely a reflection of his individual prowess but also of the synergy he had developed with his team. The chemistry between players can often be the difference between victory and defeat, and in Apex's case, it was a catalyst for success.

The Emergence of a Star

Apex's gameplay style, characterized by aggressive entry fragging, became a topic of discussion among esports commentators. The term "entry fragger" refers to the player who takes the lead in engagements, often risking their own life to secure the first kill and create opportunities for teammates. This role is critical in setting the pace of a match. Apex's ability to read opponents and exploit weaknesses set him apart from his peers.

$$\text{Entry Fragging Success} = \text{First Kills} \times \text{Impact Factor} \tag{17}$$

During the GEC, Apex achieved a staggering number of first kills, which significantly boosted his *Impact Factor*, a metric that quantifies a player's influence on the game's outcome. This performance not only solidified his reputation but also garnered attention from major esports organizations.

International Tournaments and Exposure

Following the GEC, invitations to prestigious international tournaments began to flood in. Apex found himself competing in the **World Esports Cup** and the **International Gaming League**, where he faced off against legendary players and teams. Each match was a stepping stone, a chance to showcase his skills on a platform that reached millions of viewers worldwide.

The media coverage of these events played a crucial role in amplifying Apex's visibility. Interviews, highlight reels, and social media buzz transformed him from a local star to a global sensation. The phenomenon of esports streaming allowed fans to witness his gameplay in real-time, creating a community of supporters who rallied behind him.

Challenges and Recognition

However, with great recognition came immense pressure. The expectations from fans and sponsors began to mount, leading to a unique set of challenges. Apex had to navigate the treacherous waters of public scrutiny while maintaining peak performance. This was a common plight among rising stars, as the weight of fame can sometimes overshadow the joy of competition.

To cope with these pressures, Apex relied on a combination of mindfulness techniques and a strong support network. Engaging with fellow players and mental health professionals became essential in managing the stress that accompanied his newfound fame.

Cultural Impact and Legacy

As his recognition grew, so did his influence within the esports community. Apex became a role model for aspiring gamers, particularly in France, where his story resonated deeply. He leveraged his platform to advocate for mental health awareness in gaming, emphasizing the importance of resilience and support.

The cultural impact of Apex's rise cannot be understated. He not only inspired a generation of gamers but also contributed to the evolving narrative of esports as a legitimate career path. The respect he garnered from peers and fans alike positioned him as a cultural icon, bridging the gap between gaming and mainstream recognition.

$$\text{Cultural Impact} = \frac{\text{Followers}}{\text{Negative Press}} \qquad (18)$$

Through strategic engagement with fans and a commitment to authenticity, Apex managed to maintain a positive image, which further solidified his legacy in the esports world.

In conclusion, gaining recognition on the international stage was not merely a series of fortunate events for Apex; it was the result of hard work, strategic play, and an unwavering commitment to his craft. As he continued to dominate the competitive scene, his journey served as a testament to the power of perseverance and the ever-expanding horizons of esports.

Establishing Himself as a Top Fragger

The journey of Anjali Esposito, known in the gaming world as Apex, was not merely a path paved with victories and accolades; it was a crucible of relentless practice, strategic evolution, and the cultivation of a distinct identity as a top fragger. To comprehend the magnitude of Apex's rise, one must delve into the intricate tapestry of skill development, game mechanics, and the psychological fortitude required to thrive in the hyper-competitive arena of esports.

Understanding the Role of a Top Fragger

In the realm of competitive gaming, particularly within first-person shooters (FPS), the term "top fragger" refers to a player who consistently achieves the highest number of eliminations in matches. This role is pivotal, as it directly correlates with a team's success. The mathematical representation of a player's impact can be expressed through the equation:

$$\text{Impact Score} = \frac{\text{Total Eliminations}}{\text{Total Deaths}} \times \text{Team Win Rate} \qquad (19)$$

Apex's journey to establishing himself as a top fragger involved mastering this equation, where not only the number of eliminations mattered but also the ability to stay alive long enough to contribute to his team's objectives.

Developing a Signature Playstyle

Apex's ascent was marked by the development of a signature playstyle that combined aggressive tactics with strategic foresight. He embraced the concept of *entry fragging*, a role that entails being the first player to engage the enemy, often leading the charge into battle. This position demands not only exceptional aiming skills but also an acute awareness of map dynamics and enemy positioning.

- **Aiming Precision:** Apex honed his aiming skills through countless hours of practice, utilizing aim trainers and engaging in scrimmages that simulated high-pressure scenarios.

- **Map Knowledge:** Understanding the intricacies of each map allowed Apex to predict enemy movements and exploit weaknesses. He studied choke points, high ground advantages, and common hiding spots, which became second nature.

- **Communication:** Apex recognized the importance of teamwork and developed a communication style that was both assertive and informative, ensuring his teammates were always in the loop regarding enemy locations and strategies.

Early Tournament Successes

The fruits of Apex's labor began to manifest during early tournaments, where his performance consistently placed him among the top players. Notably, during the *International Esports Championship*, Apex's team secured a remarkable victory, with him achieving an astonishing average of 25 eliminations per match. This success was not merely a stroke of luck; it was a testament to his preparation and skill.

Gaining Recognition on the International Stage

As Apex's reputation grew, so did the scrutiny. Competing at the highest levels of esports brought not only accolades but also intense pressure. The psychological aspect of maintaining peak performance became increasingly significant. Apex employed various techniques to manage this pressure, including:

1. **Mental Conditioning:** Regular sessions with sports psychologists helped him develop mental resilience, enabling him to remain calm and focused during high-stakes matches.

2. **Visualization Techniques:** Apex practiced visualization, mentally rehearsing his gameplay to enhance his decision-making speed during actual matches.

3. **Physical Fitness:** Recognizing the connection between physical health and mental acuity, Apex incorporated fitness routines into his regimen, improving his overall stamina and concentration.

Establishing Himself as a Top Fragger

The culmination of Apex's efforts was his establishment as a top fragger, a title not easily earned in the world of esports. He achieved this through a combination of skill, strategy, and sheer determination. His statistics began to reflect his prowess, as he consistently led his team in eliminations, contributing to their overall success and solidifying his place in the annals of esports history.

In conclusion, the journey of Anjali Esposito, or Apex, from a passionate gamer to a top fragger is a narrative of dedication, skill refinement, and the relentless pursuit of excellence. His story serves as an inspiration to aspiring gamers, illustrating that with the right mindset and preparation, the pinnacle of success in esports is within reach.

Behind the Gamer Tag

The Story Behind the Name

In the vast and electrifying universe of esports, names can be more than mere identifiers; they are a tapestry woven with ambition, persona, and legacy. For Anjali Esposito, known in the competitive gaming arena as "Apex," the origin of this moniker is steeped in a blend of personal significance and strategic branding—a narrative that echoes the very essence of his journey.

The name "Apex" conjures images of peaks and pinnacles, symbolizing the highest point of achievement and excellence. This choice was not arbitrary; it was a deliberate reflection of Anjali's aspirations. From an early age, he was drawn to the idea of reaching the summit of competitive gaming, a goal that seemed daunting yet exhilarating. The term "apex" resonated with his desire to be at the forefront of the esports scene, leading the charge as a fierce entry fragger—a role that demands not only skill but also courage and tenacity.

The genesis of the name can be traced back to a pivotal moment in Anjali's formative years. As a young gamer, he often found himself captivated by the thrill of competition, immersing himself in various titles that demanded quick reflexes and strategic thinking. During a particularly intense gaming session with friends, Anjali executed a series of flawless plays that turned the tide of the match. In the heat of the moment, one of his friends exclaimed, "You're like the apex predator out there!" This metaphor struck a chord, encapsulating Anjali's competitive spirit and his knack for dominating the battlefield.

However, the journey to adopting the name "Apex" was not without its challenges. In the early days of his gaming career, Anjali faced skepticism from peers and critics alike. Many questioned whether a name so bold could be backed by actual skill. This external pressure only fueled his determination. He embraced the moniker as a badge of honor, vowing to embody the qualities it represented: precision, agility, and a relentless pursuit of greatness.

In the realm of esports, where branding can make or break a player's career, the name "Apex" also served a practical purpose. It was short, memorable, and evocative—qualities that are essential in an industry where first impressions are often made in a matter of seconds. Anjali understood that to stand out in a crowded field, he needed a name that would stick in the minds of fans and opponents alike. Thus, "Apex" became not just a name but a brand, one that would carry him through the trials and triumphs of his career.

As Anjali began to make a name for himself in the competitive scene, the significance of his chosen identity deepened. He became synonymous with aggressive gameplay and strategic prowess, embodying the very essence of what it meant to be an entry fragger. The name "Apex" transformed into a rallying cry for fans, a symbol of resilience and skill that inspired a new generation of gamers.

Moreover, the importance of identity in esports cannot be overstated. Players often find themselves navigating the complexities of public perception, fan expectations, and personal authenticity. Anjali's journey with the name "Apex" exemplifies this dynamic. It became a crucial part of his narrative, allowing him to connect with his audience on a deeper level. Fans resonated with the idea of striving for the apex, not just in gaming but in life—a universal theme that transcends the digital realm.

As Apex continued to rise through the ranks, the name took on a life of its own. It became a cultural icon within the esports community, representing not just Anjali's individual achievements but also the collective aspirations of aspiring gamers worldwide. The persona of Apex evolved, embodying the dreams and hopes of those who dared to challenge the status quo.

In conclusion, the story behind the name "Apex" is a testament to Anjali Esposito's journey—a narrative woven with ambition, resilience, and the relentless pursuit of excellence. It is a name that encapsulates the essence of competitive gaming, serving as a beacon for those who aspire to reach their own apex in the world of esports. As we delve further into the life and legacy of Apex, it becomes evident that this name is more than just a label; it is a symbol of a storied career marked by trials, triumphs, and an unwavering commitment to becoming the best.

The Importance of Identity in Esports

In the world of esports, identity transcends mere personal branding; it becomes a vital component of an athlete's success and influence within the competitive landscape. The concept of identity encompasses not only the gamer's name and persona but also their playstyle, values, and the community they represent. This multifaceted identity shapes how players are perceived by fans, sponsors, and the broader gaming community.

Theoretical Framework

The importance of identity in esports can be analyzed through various theoretical lenses, including social identity theory and the concept of self-branding. Social identity theory posits that individuals derive a sense of self from their group memberships, which in esports can include teams, gaming genres, and even fandoms. According to Tajfel and Turner (1979), the categorization of oneself within a social group enhances self-esteem and fosters a sense of belonging.

In the context of esports, players often adopt a gamer tag that resonates with their personality or gaming style, creating a distinct identity that fans can rally behind. This identity is not static; it evolves over time as players gain experience, face challenges, and adapt to the ever-changing landscape of competitive gaming.

Challenges of Identity Formation

However, the formation and maintenance of a strong identity in esports come with challenges. Players often face pressure to conform to the expectations of their teams, sponsors, and fanbases. This pressure can lead to an identity crisis, where the athlete struggles to balance their personal values with external demands. For example, a player may feel compelled to adopt a more aggressive playstyle to fit the team's strategy, potentially alienating their original fanbase who appreciated their unique approach.

Moreover, the rapid pace of change in the esports industry can render established identities obsolete. As new games emerge and trends shift, players must continuously adapt their identities to remain relevant. This dynamic environment can create a sense of instability, making it crucial for athletes to cultivate a flexible and resilient identity.

Identity as a Tool for Inspiration

Despite these challenges, a well-crafted identity can serve as a powerful tool for inspiration and community building. Apex, for instance, has cultivated an identity that resonates with aspiring gamers, embodying the spirit of perseverance and excellence. His gamer tag, "Apex," symbolizes not just a peak performance but also the aspiration to rise above challenges. This identity has inspired countless young gamers to pursue their dreams, demonstrating the ripple effect of a strong personal brand.

Moreover, identity plays a significant role in marketing and sponsorship opportunities. Brands are increasingly looking for athletes whose identities align with their values and target audiences. A player's identity can enhance their marketability, leading to lucrative sponsorship deals and collaborations. For instance, Apex's commitment to mental health awareness and community engagement has attracted brands that prioritize social responsibility, thereby reinforcing his identity as not just a gamer but also a role model.

Case Studies: Successful Identity Management

Several esports athletes have successfully navigated the complexities of identity in their careers. One notable example is Faker, the legendary League of Legends player, whose identity is closely tied to his exceptional skill and sportsmanship. Faker's consistent performance and humble demeanor have made him a beloved figure in the esports community, illustrating how a positive identity can foster loyalty and admiration.

Conversely, the story of a player who faced backlash due to a controversial incident highlights the fragility of identity in esports. When a well-known player was involved in a scandal, their identity as a respected athlete was called into question, leading to a significant loss of sponsorships and fan support. This incident underscores the importance of maintaining a positive and authentic identity, as missteps can have lasting repercussions.

Conclusion

In conclusion, the importance of identity in esports cannot be overstated. It serves as a foundation for personal branding, community engagement, and professional success. As players navigate the complexities of their identities, they must remain mindful of the impact their choices have on their careers and the communities they represent. A strong, authentic identity not only enhances a player's marketability but also inspires the next generation of gamers to forge their paths in the dynamic world of esports. The journey of identity formation is ongoing, and those who embrace their true selves while adapting to the ever-evolving landscape will undoubtedly leave a lasting legacy in the esports arena.

Embracing the Persona of Apex

In the vibrant realm of esports, where digital avatars often transcend the physical identities of players, the persona of an athlete can become as crucial as their skillset. For Anjali Esposito, known to the world as Apex, this transformation into a larger-than-life character was not merely a strategic choice but a necessary evolution in the pursuit of greatness.

The essence of Apex is deeply rooted in the fusion of his gaming prowess and the carefully crafted persona that resonates with fans and competitors alike. The character embodies not just a name, but a narrative—a story of resilience, triumph, and fierce competition. This section explores the multifaceted nature of Apex's persona and its implications within the esports landscape.

The Anatomy of a Persona

Apex's persona can be dissected into several key components, each contributing to the overall image that fans have come to adore. Theoretical frameworks such as Goffman's *Presentation of Self in Everyday Life* provide a lens through which we can understand the construction of identity in performance settings. In the case of Apex, the following elements play a pivotal role:

- **Authenticity:** Apex's persona is rooted in his genuine passion for gaming. Unlike many who adopt a façade, Anjali's character is an extension of his true self, which fosters a deeper connection with his audience.

- **Charisma:** The ability to engage and captivate an audience is paramount. Apex's charisma stems from his dynamic playstyle and his interactions with fans, which are often characterized by wit and an approachable demeanor.

- **Narrative:** The story of Apex—from humble beginnings to becoming a top fragger—creates a compelling narrative that resonates with aspiring gamers. This narrative is not just about victories but also about the struggles and setbacks faced along the way.

The Power of Branding

Apex's persona is not merely an identity; it is a brand. In the competitive world of esports, branding is essential for differentiation and marketability. Apex has successfully leveraged his persona to create a recognizable brand that extends beyond gameplay. This branding includes:

$$\text{Brand Equity} = \text{Perceived Quality} + \text{Brand Loyalty} + \text{Brand Awareness} \quad (20)$$

Where: - *Perceived Quality* reflects the audience's perception of Apex's gaming skills. - *Brand Loyalty* represents the dedication of his fan base. - *Brand Awareness* indicates how well the name Apex is recognized in the esports community.

Apex's brand is characterized by its vibrant visual identity, including logos, merchandise, and social media presence. These elements are crucial in maintaining a cohesive image that fans can rally behind.

The Impact of Persona on Performance

The persona of Apex has tangible effects on his performance. Psychological theories suggest that embodying a persona can enhance confidence and reduce anxiety, crucial elements in high-stakes gaming environments. The concept of *self-efficacy*, as proposed by Bandura, plays a significant role here:

$$\text{Self-Efficacy} = \frac{\text{Successes}}{\text{Failures} + \text{Successes}} \quad (21)$$

This equation illustrates that as Apex experiences more successes, his self-efficacy increases, further solidifying his persona and performance.

Moreover, the persona of Apex allows him to cope with the pressures of competition. By embracing this character, he creates a psychological buffer that enables him to navigate the intense scrutiny and expectations that accompany fame in esports.

Inspiring a New Generation

Apex's persona has become a beacon of inspiration for budding gamers. By embracing his identity, he has opened doors for discussions about self-expression and authenticity within the esports community. The impact of this persona is evident in the way it encourages young players to cultivate their unique identities rather than conforming to a singular mold.

In interviews and public appearances, Apex often emphasizes the importance of being true to oneself and the value of perseverance. This message resonates deeply, particularly in a field where many face challenges related to mental health and societal expectations. By sharing his journey, Apex becomes not just a player but a mentor—a guiding light for those navigating their paths in the esports universe.

The Future of Apex's Persona

As Apex continues to evolve, so too does his persona. The dynamic nature of esports means that identities can shift and adapt in response to changing landscapes. Apex's ability to embrace this evolution while maintaining the core elements of his character will be crucial in sustaining his relevance and influence.

In conclusion, the persona of Apex is a complex interplay of authenticity, branding, and psychological resilience. It serves as a testament to the power of identity in esports, illustrating that behind every gamer tag lies a story waiting to be told. As Anjali Esposito continues to carve his legacy, the persona of Apex will undoubtedly remain a pivotal aspect of his journey—one that inspires, captivates, and resonates with fans across the globe.

Inspiring a New Generation of Gamers

In the ever-evolving landscape of esports, few figures shine as brightly as Anjali Esposito, known to the world as Apex. His journey from a passionate gamer to a celebrated entry fragger has not only carved a niche for himself in the competitive gaming scene but has also ignited a spark of inspiration in countless aspiring gamers. The essence of Apex's influence lies in his ability to transcend the role of a mere player; he embodies the spirit of resilience, creativity, and innovation that resonates deeply with the youth of today.

The Power of Representation

Representation plays a pivotal role in shaping the aspirations of young gamers. Apex's ascent to fame has provided a tangible example for aspiring players, particularly those from underrepresented backgrounds. His story illustrates that success in esports is attainable, regardless of one's origins or challenges faced along the way. This notion is supported by social cognitive theory, which posits that individuals learn and are motivated by observing others. Apex's visibility in the esports community serves as a powerful motivator for many, encouraging them to pursue their passions and overcome obstacles.

Mentorship and Community Engagement

Apex has actively engaged with the gaming community, offering mentorship and guidance to budding players. Through streaming platforms and social media, he shares insights into his gameplay, strategies, and the mental fortitude required to excel in competitive environments. This direct interaction fosters a sense of community, where aspiring gamers can learn from a seasoned professional. Research indicates that mentorship significantly enhances the learning curve for novices, as it provides them with personalized feedback and encouragement (Ragins, 1997). Apex's willingness to invest time in nurturing talent exemplifies the importance of mentorship in esports.

Innovative Playstyles and Strategies

One of the hallmarks of Apex's gameplay is his unique approach to entry fragging. His signature playstyle, characterized by aggressive yet calculated movements, has set a benchmark for aspiring gamers. By demonstrating the effectiveness of innovative strategies, Apex challenges the status quo and encourages others to think outside the box. The concept of "creative destruction" in economics can be applied here; just as new ideas disrupt established norms, Apex's gameplay inspires a generation to break free from conventional tactics and explore new possibilities.

Building a Brand and Personal Identity

Apex's journey is not solely about in-game achievements; it also encompasses the cultivation of a personal brand. He has adeptly navigated the complexities of branding in esports, establishing himself as a cultural icon. By embracing his identity and sharing his story, Apex encourages young gamers to develop their unique personas. The importance of personal branding in the digital age cannot be overstated; it empowers individuals to create a narrative that resonates with their audience, fostering a deeper connection with fans and aspiring players alike.

The Role of Mental Health Awareness

Inspiring a new generation of gamers also involves addressing the often-overlooked aspect of mental health. Apex has been vocal about his struggles with anxiety and the importance of mental wellness in esports. By openly discussing these issues, he destigmatizes mental health challenges and encourages young players to prioritize their well-being. Research shows that mental health significantly impacts performance in high-stress environments (Kreiner et al., 2020). Apex's advocacy for mental health awareness serves as a crucial reminder that success is not solely defined by victories but also by maintaining a healthy balance in life.

The Legacy of Apex

Apex's influence extends beyond his gameplay; he is a beacon of hope and motivation for a generation of gamers. His journey illustrates that with passion, dedication, and resilience, one can rise above challenges and achieve greatness. As he continues to inspire young players, Apex is not merely shaping the future of esports; he is cultivating a culture of inclusivity, creativity, and mental wellness. The legacy he is building will undoubtedly resonate for years to come, empowering future generations to chase their dreams fearlessly.

In conclusion, Apex embodies the essence of what it means to be a role model in the esports realm. His commitment to inspiring others through representation, mentorship, innovative strategies, personal branding, and mental health advocacy sets a powerful example for aspiring gamers. As the esports landscape continues to evolve, the impact of figures like Apex will be felt long after the final match has been played, lighting the path for the next generation of gaming legends.

Becoming a Cultural Icon

In the ever-evolving landscape of esports, few figures have transcended the confines of their digital realms to become cultural icons quite like Anjali Esposito, known to the world as Apex. His journey from a passionate gamer to a household name mirrors the rise of esports itself, reflecting broader cultural shifts that have transformed the gaming community into a vibrant subculture. This section explores the multifaceted dimensions of Apex's ascent to cultural icon status, examining the interplay between identity, community, and the transformative power of digital platforms.

The Intersection of Gaming and Culture

Apex's impact extends beyond mere gameplay; he embodies the fusion of gaming with contemporary culture. The phenomenon of gaming as a cultural force can be analyzed through the lens of cultural studies, where theorists like Stuart Hall argue that cultural icons serve as sites of negotiation between various social identities. Apex's persona resonates with a diverse audience, as he navigates issues of gender, race, and class within the gaming community. His identity as a fierce entry fragger challenges traditional stereotypes associated with gamers, positioning him as a role model for aspiring players across the globe.

The Role of Media and Representation

Media representation plays a crucial role in the construction of cultural icons. Apex's visibility on platforms like Twitch and YouTube has allowed him to cultivate a personal brand that resonates with millions. His streams, filled with charisma and skillful gameplay, have not only entertained but also educated his audience about the intricacies of competitive gaming. The power of digital media in shaping public perception cannot be overstated; as theorist Henry Jenkins posits, participatory culture enables fans to engage with content creators in ways that were previously unimaginable. Apex's active engagement with his fanbase fosters a sense of community, elevating him to a status that transcends the confines of traditional celebrity.

Inspiring a New Generation

Apex's influence is particularly evident in his role as a mentor and inspiration to a new generation of gamers. His journey serves as a testament to the idea that success in esports is attainable, regardless of background. By sharing his experiences—both triumphs and tribulations—Apex empowers aspiring players to pursue their passions. This mentorship extends beyond gameplay; it encompasses discussions about mental health, resilience, and the importance of support networks in the gaming community. The cultural significance of this mentorship is profound, as it challenges the notion that gaming is a solitary endeavor, instead highlighting the collaborative spirit that defines esports.

The Cultural Impact of the "Apex Effect"

The phenomenon known as the "Apex Effect" encapsulates the broader cultural implications of his success. This term refers to the ripple effect of Apex's achievements, which inspire not only individual players but also entire communities. The Apex Effect can be modeled through social network theory, where the connections formed within the gaming community amplify the impact of individual successes. In this context, Apex's victories serve as catalysts for change, motivating others to strive for excellence and fostering a culture of inclusivity and diversity within esports.

Challenges of Fame and Cultural Responsibility

However, with great power comes great responsibility. As Apex navigates the complexities of fame, he faces the dual challenge of maintaining his authenticity while fulfilling the expectations of his fans. The pressure to embody the ideals of a cultural icon can lead to mental strain, as highlighted by the struggles many esports athletes face with mental health. Apex's openness about his own challenges serves as a vital reminder of the importance of mental wellness in the gaming community. By addressing these issues, he not only humanizes the experience of being a professional gamer but also reinforces the notion that cultural icons have a responsibility to advocate for positive change.

Legacy and Future Influence

In conclusion, Apex's journey to becoming a cultural icon reflects the dynamic interplay between gaming and culture. His impact is felt not only in the realm of esports but also in the broader cultural landscape, where he serves as a beacon of hope and inspiration. As he continues to evolve, the legacy of Apex will undoubtedly shape the future of competitive gaming, inspiring generations to come to embrace their identities and pursue their passions. The cultural icon status he has achieved is not merely a product of his skill but a testament to the power of community, representation, and the relentless pursuit of excellence in the world of esports.

$$\text{Cultural Impact} = \text{Visibility} \times \text{Engagement} \times \text{Representation} \tag{22}$$

This equation encapsulates the essence of Apex's influence, illustrating how these interconnected factors contribute to his status as a cultural icon in the esports arena.

The Impact on the Esports Industry

The emergence of Anjali Esposito, known by her gamer tag "Apex," has left an indelible mark on the esports industry, reshaping perceptions and paving the way for future generations of gamers. Apex's rise to fame is not merely a personal triumph; it represents a seismic shift in how esports athletes are viewed, valued, and integrated into the broader cultural landscape.

Redefining Professionalism

Apex's professional conduct and dedication have set new standards within the esports community. Traditionally viewed as a niche hobby, gaming has evolved into a legitimate profession, attracting sponsorships, media attention, and a diverse audience. Apex's success underscores the importance of professionalism, discipline, and strategic thinking, qualities that are now essential for aspiring esports athletes.

This shift can be quantified through the increasing investment in esports organizations. According to [?], global esports revenues are projected to surpass $1.8 billion by 2024, illustrating the financial viability of the industry. Apex's achievements have catalyzed this growth, attracting sponsors eager to align themselves with successful, marketable players.

Influence on Game Development

Apex's gameplay style and strategic innovations have not only influenced her team but also impacted game developers. The meta—the evolving strategies and tactics that define competitive play—has been significantly shaped by her approach. For instance, her aggressive entry fragging style has led to adjustments in character balancing and game mechanics by developers seeking to maintain competitive integrity.

Developers have taken note of the dynamics introduced by players like Apex, leading to the incorporation of community feedback into game updates. The iterative process of game development has become increasingly responsive to the competitive scene, creating a feedback loop where player performance directly influences game design.

Cultural Impact and Representation

Apex's prominence has also sparked conversations about representation and diversity within esports. As a female athlete in a predominantly male-dominated field, she has become a role model for aspiring gamers, particularly young women. Her visibility challenges stereotypes and encourages inclusivity, fostering a more welcoming environment for all players.

The cultural ramifications are profound. Apex's story has been featured in various media outlets, from documentaries to interviews, emphasizing the importance of diverse voices in gaming. This narrative shift is crucial, as it not only highlights the achievements of female gamers but also inspires a broader audience to engage with esports.

The Rise of Fan Engagement

Apex's influence extends to fan engagement, transforming how players interact with their audiences. Through social media platforms and streaming services, she has cultivated a loyal fanbase that transcends traditional fandom. The concept of the "streamer-athlete" has emerged, where players like Apex connect with fans on a personal level, sharing insights, gameplay strategies, and even personal anecdotes.

This direct engagement fosters a sense of community, allowing fans to feel invested in the success of their favorite players. Apex's ability to navigate this landscape has set a precedent for how athletes can leverage their platforms for both personal branding and community building.

Addressing Challenges in the Industry

Despite the positive impact of Apex on the esports industry, challenges remain. Issues such as toxicity, mental health, and burnout continue to plague the community. Apex's candid discussions about her struggles with mental health have brought these issues to the forefront, encouraging open dialogue and promoting mental wellness initiatives within esports organizations.

The equation for success in this context can be expressed as:

$$\text{Success} = \text{Skill} + \text{Mental Health} + \text{Community Support}$$

This formula highlights the multifaceted nature of success in esports, emphasizing that while skill is vital, mental health and community support are equally important for sustainable performance.

Conclusion

In conclusion, Anjali Esposito, through her journey as Apex, has not only redefined what it means to be a professional esports athlete but has also catalyzed significant changes in the industry. Her impact resonates across multiple facets—professionalism, game development, cultural representation, fan engagement, and addressing industry challenges. As the esports landscape continues to evolve, Apex's legacy will undoubtedly inspire future generations of gamers to push boundaries, challenge norms, and strive for excellence in this dynamic arena.

Dealing with Fame and Fan Expectations

Fame in the esports realm can be as exhilarating as it is daunting. For Anjali Esposito, known in the gaming world as Apex, the sudden surge of popularity brought with it a cascade of expectations from fans, sponsors, and the esports community at large. Navigating this treacherous landscape required a delicate balance between personal authenticity and the persona crafted for public consumption.

The Weight of Expectations

As Apex's star began to rise, so too did the expectations surrounding his performance. Fans often projected their desires onto him, expecting not only consistent victories but also a flawless representation of what an esports athlete should embody. This phenomenon can be understood through the lens of *social comparison theory*, which posits that individuals determine their own social and personal worth based on how they stack up against others. For Apex, every match became a metric by which fans measured not just his skill, but his worth as a competitor and a role model.

The Pressure Cooker of Performance

The pressure to perform can be likened to a pressure cooker; without proper management, it can lead to catastrophic failures. Apex faced this pressure head-on, often feeling as though he was living under a microscope. The constant scrutiny from fans and analysts alike created a scenario where even minor mistakes were magnified, leading to a cycle of anxiety and self-doubt. The psychological toll of this scrutiny is significant, as illustrated by the equation:

$$P = \frac{F}{E}$$

where P is the pressure felt by the athlete, F is the force of fan expectations, and E is the athlete's ability to cope with those expectations. As Apex's popularity grew, the force F increased, often outpacing his coping mechanisms E.

Navigating Fan Interactions

Apex's approach to dealing with fame involved a strategic engagement with his fanbase. He recognized that while fans could be a source of immense support, they could also be a double-edged sword. The interaction with fans, particularly through social media platforms, became a vital part of his strategy. By sharing behind-the-scenes glimpses of his life and gaming experiences, Apex was able to humanize himself, creating a connection that transcended mere fandom.

However, this engagement also came with its own set of challenges. The immediacy of social media meant that negative comments and criticisms could reach him instantaneously. Apex learned to filter this feedback, focusing on constructive criticism while disregarding toxic negativity. This is where the concept of *emotional resilience* comes into play, allowing him to bounce back from setbacks and maintain a positive outlook.

Balancing Personal and Professional Life

The line between personal life and professional obligations often blurred for Apex. As fame enveloped him, he found it increasingly difficult to carve out time for personal pursuits and relationships. The pressure to constantly engage with fans and maintain a public persona can lead to burnout, as noted in the theory of *role conflict*. Apex had to navigate the conflicting demands of his public persona as a gaming icon and his private self, which craved normalcy and downtime.

To combat this, Apex implemented strict boundaries regarding his time and availability. He dedicated specific hours for streaming and fan interaction, ensuring that he also carved out personal time to recharge. This balance was crucial in maintaining his mental health and sustaining his performance levels in competitions.

Lessons Learned

Through the trials of fame, Apex gleaned several important lessons. Firstly, he learned the value of authenticity. Fans appreciate genuine interactions over curated responses. Secondly, he recognized the importance of mental health, advocating for open conversations about mental wellness within the esports community. Lastly, Apex understood that while he could not control fan expectations, he could control his response to them, ultimately shaping his narrative rather than allowing it to be dictated by others.

In conclusion, dealing with fame and fan expectations is a complex endeavor for any esports athlete. For Apex, it has been a journey of self-discovery, resilience, and growth. By embracing his identity, setting boundaries, and fostering genuine connections with his fans, he has not only navigated the challenges of fame but has also inspired others to do the same. The lessons learned from his experiences serve as a beacon for aspiring esports athletes, illuminating the path through the often tumultuous waters of fame.

Balancing Personal and Professional Life

In the fast-paced world of esports, where the line between personal and professional life often blurs, finding a harmonious balance becomes an intricate dance. For Anjali Esposito, known by her gamer tag "Apex," this balancing act is not merely a challenge;

it is a fundamental aspect of her journey that shapes her both as an athlete and as a person.

The Duality of Life

As a professional esports athlete, Apex is constantly thrust into the spotlight. The demands of training, competition, and public appearances can be overwhelming. The pressure to perform at the highest level often leads to a neglect of personal well-being. According to [?], the duality of life for esports athletes presents unique challenges that can lead to burnout if not managed properly.

The equation that encapsulates this struggle can be represented as:

$$B = P + C - S \qquad (23)$$

Where:

- B = Balance

- P = Personal life satisfaction

- C = Career demands

- S = Stress levels

In Apex's case, the challenge lies in maximizing P while minimizing C and S. This balancing act requires a keen awareness of her mental and emotional state, as well as proactive strategies to mitigate stress.

Setting Boundaries

One of the first steps Apex took to achieve balance was to establish clear boundaries between her professional commitments and personal time. This involved setting specific hours for practice and competition while reserving time for relaxation, hobbies, and social interactions.

Apex often emphasizes the importance of this boundary-setting in her interviews. She once stated, "You can't be a great player if you're not a whole person. Taking time for myself is just as crucial as grinding for hours on end." This philosophy aligns with the findings of [?], which suggest that personal time enhances overall performance in high-pressure environments.

The Role of Support Systems

Apex's journey also highlights the significance of a supportive network. Her friends, family, and teammates play a pivotal role in her ability to maintain balance. They provide emotional support, encouragement, and a sense of normalcy amidst the chaos of competitive gaming.

Research by [?] indicates that social support can significantly reduce stress and enhance resilience in athletes. Apex's reliance on her support system exemplifies this theory. For instance, during a particularly challenging tournament season, she leaned on her family for emotional support, which helped her regain focus and motivation.

Mindfulness and Self-Care

Incorporating mindfulness practices into her routine has also been a game-changer for Apex. Techniques such as meditation, yoga, and journaling allow her to center herself and manage stress effectively. These practices not only improve her mental health but also enhance her performance in-game.

Apex often shares her mindfulness journey with her followers, stating, "When I take a moment to breathe and reflect, I can see the bigger picture. It helps me stay grounded, especially when the pressure is on." This sentiment resonates with the growing body of literature that supports mindfulness as a tool for athletes to enhance focus and reduce anxiety [?].

The Challenge of Fame

However, the fame that comes with being a top esports athlete adds another layer of complexity to balancing personal and professional life. The expectations from fans, sponsors, and the media can be relentless. Apex has faced moments where her personal life was scrutinized, leading to increased stress and anxiety.

To combat this, she has learned to manage her public persona carefully, often sharing curated glimpses of her life while keeping certain aspects private. This selective sharing allows her to maintain a sense of privacy and autonomy, crucial for her mental well-being.

Conclusion

In conclusion, balancing personal and professional life is an ongoing journey for Apex. By setting boundaries, relying on her support system, incorporating mindfulness, and managing the pressures of fame, she navigates the complexities of her dual existence. As she continues to inspire a new generation of gamers, her story serves as a reminder that achieving balance is not just about success in the arena but about cultivating a fulfilling life beyond the screen.

"The Apex Effect"

The phenomenon known as "The Apex Effect" embodies the profound impact that Anjali Esposito, widely known by her gamer tag Apex, has had on the esports landscape. This effect transcends mere statistics and accolades; it encapsulates the cultural, psychological, and strategic shifts instigated by her presence in the competitive gaming arena.

The Cultural Shift

Apex's rise to prominence coincided with a pivotal moment in esports history. As gaming transitioned from a niche hobby to a global spectacle, Apex emerged as a beacon for aspiring gamers. Her unique playstyle, characterized by aggressive entry fragging, not only set a new standard for professional gameplay but also inspired a legion of fans and future competitors.

The cultural ramifications of her success are evident in the increased visibility of female gamers in a predominantly male-dominated space. Apex's achievements challenged stereotypes and encouraged diversity within the esports community.

Psychological Impact

The psychological implications of "The Apex Effect" are equally significant. Apex's journey through adversity, including mental health struggles and team conflicts, resonates with many in the gaming community. Her openness about battling anxiety and depression has fostered a dialogue about mental wellness in esports.

Apex's mantra, "Play with passion, not pressure," serves as a guiding principle for many players. This perspective emphasizes the importance of maintaining mental health while striving for excellence, a balance that is often overlooked in the competitive scene.

Strategic Innovations

From a strategic standpoint, Apex's gameplay has led to the development of new tactics within team dynamics. Her ability to read opponents and adapt in real-time has influenced how teams approach entry fragging. The mathematical model for assessing player impact can be illustrated through the following equation:

$$\text{Impact Score} = \frac{\text{Total Eliminations}}{\text{Total Deaths} + 1} \qquad (24)$$

This equation quantifies the effectiveness of an entry fragger, highlighting the importance of maintaining a high kill-to-death ratio. Apex's consistent high scores in this metric have set benchmarks for aspiring players.

The Ripple Effect

The "Apex Effect" extends beyond individual gameplay. It has catalyzed changes within team structures and coaching methodologies. Teams are now more inclined to invest in psychological support and training, recognizing that mental fortitude is as crucial as technical skill.

For example, the implementation of sports psychology sessions in training regimens has become commonplace. Teams that adopt these practices often see improved performance and cohesion, as players learn to manage stress and work collaboratively under pressure.

Inspiring Future Generations

Perhaps the most enduring aspect of "The Apex Effect" is its potential to inspire future generations of gamers. Apex's story is one of perseverance, resilience, and triumph against the odds. Her journey emphasizes that success in esports is not solely about talent; it is also about determination, adaptability, and the willingness to learn from failures.

The creation of initiatives aimed at nurturing young talent, such as mentorship programs and scholarship opportunities, can be traced back to Apex's influence. These programs aim to provide aspiring gamers with the resources and support necessary to succeed, ensuring that the next wave of esports athletes is equipped to navigate the challenges of competitive gaming.

Conclusion

In conclusion, "The Apex Effect" is a multifaceted phenomenon that encompasses cultural shifts, psychological insights, strategic innovations, and a commitment to nurturing future talent. Apex's legacy is not merely about her victories; it is about the profound changes she has inspired within the esports community. As we continue to witness the evolution of competitive gaming, the impact of Apex will undoubtedly resonate for years to come, shaping the landscape for aspiring players and fans alike.

"The Apex Effect"

The phenomenon known as "The Apex Effect" encapsulates the transformative influence that Anjali Esposito, better known by his gamer tag Apex, has had on the esports landscape. This section seeks to explore the various dimensions of this effect, including its implications on player performance, team dynamics, and the broader gaming culture.

Defining the Apex Effect

At its core, "The Apex Effect" refers to the heightened performance and morale that players experience when competing alongside or against Apex. This effect can be understood through the lens of social facilitation theory, which posits that the presence of others can enhance an individual's performance on simple tasks. In the context of esports, the presence of a high-caliber player like Apex can elevate the performance levels of his teammates, fostering a competitive yet supportive environment.

$$P = f(T, E) \tag{25}$$

Where P represents performance, T denotes team dynamics, and E signifies the external environment, including factors like audience engagement and media attention. Apex's presence often shifts the values of T and E significantly, leading to improved performance outcomes.

The Psychological Impact

The Apex Effect is not merely a statistical phenomenon; it also has profound psychological implications. Players who have the opportunity to play with or against Apex often report increased motivation and a sense of urgency to improve their skills. This can be attributed to the concept of vicarious reinforcement, where observing a skilled player can inspire others to push their limits.

$$M = R + C \tag{26}$$

Where M is motivation, R is the reinforcement received from observing Apex's gameplay, and C is the competitive spirit ignited by the challenge of facing a top-tier player. This dynamic creates a feedback loop that not only enhances individual performance but also contributes to the overall success of the team.

Examples of the Apex Effect in Action

Several instances throughout Apex's career illustrate the tangible effects of his presence on team performance. One notable example occurred during the Intel Championship, where Apex's leadership and skill propelled his team to victory against formidable opponents. The synergy created by his gameplay style, characterized by aggressive entry fragging and strategic positioning, set a benchmark for others to emulate.

In a post-match interview, his teammate remarked, "Playing alongside Apex is like having a cheat code. He elevates everyone's game." This sentiment echoes the experiences of many players who have felt the motivational surge that accompanies competing with a legend.

The Cultural Shift in Esports

Beyond individual and team performance, "The Apex Effect" has instigated a cultural shift within the esports community. His rise to prominence has inspired a new generation of gamers to pursue competitive play, leading to an influx of players who aspire to emulate his success. This phenomenon can be analyzed through the lens of social learning theory, which emphasizes the role of observation and imitation in learning behaviors.

$$B = O + I \qquad (27)$$

Where B is behavior, O is the observed behavior of Apex, and I represents individual initiative to incorporate those behaviors into their own gameplay. The result is a burgeoning community of aspiring entry fraggers who seek to replicate Apex's techniques and mindset.

The Lasting Legacy of the Apex Effect

As Apex continues to compete and innovate, the legacy of "The Apex Effect" will undoubtedly endure. His contributions to team strategies and game mechanics have not only influenced his contemporaries but have also laid the groundwork for future generations of esports athletes.

In conclusion, "The Apex Effect" serves as a testament to the power of individual influence in a team-oriented environment. By harnessing the psychological and social dynamics at play, Apex has not only carved out a niche for himself but has also elevated the entire esports community. This effect will resonate long after his competitive career concludes, shaping the future of gaming and the aspirations of countless players worldwide.

Trials and Triumphs

Trials and Triumphs

Trials and Triumphs

In the world of esports, where the stakes are as high as the adrenaline levels, the journey of a player is often fraught with trials and triumphs. For Anjali Esposito, known in the gaming realm as Apex, this chapter of his life was marked by defining moments that not only shaped his career but also tested his resolve and passion for competitive gaming.

The Intel Championship

The Intel Championship was not merely another tournament for Apex; it was the crucible in which his mettle was tested. The journey towards this prestigious event was paved with challenges that would have daunted even the most seasoned competitors. Apex, however, viewed these obstacles as opportunities for growth.

$$\text{Success} = \text{Hard Work} + \text{Perseverance} + \text{Skill} \tag{28}$$

This equation became a mantra for Apex, encapsulating his belief that success in esports is not solely dependent on innate talent but also on the relentless pursuit of improvement. The preparation for the Intel Championship involved countless hours of practice, strategy sessions, and scrims with his teammates, each moment a step toward the ultimate goal.

Overcoming Adversity and Mental Roadblocks

As Apex approached the championship, he faced not only physical challenges but also mental roadblocks that threatened to derail his aspirations. The pressure to perform at the highest level can be overwhelming, leading to anxiety and self-doubt.

Apex's experience was no exception. He often found himself grappling with the fear of failure, a common affliction among elite athletes. To combat this, he sought the guidance of sports psychologists who helped him develop mental resilience. Techniques such as visualization and mindfulness became integral parts of his routine, allowing him to stay focused and calm under pressure.

$$\text{Mental Resilience} = \text{Focus} + \text{Confidence} + \text{Preparation} \qquad (29)$$

This equation illustrates the components that Apex worked to strengthen, ensuring that when the moment of truth arrived, he would be ready to seize it.

The Unforgettable Victory

The culmination of Apex's hard work and mental fortitude came during the Intel Championship finals. The atmosphere was electric, filled with the cheers of fans and the palpable tension of competition. Apex and his team faced off against a formidable opponent, Team Pinnacle, known for their aggressive playstyle and strategic prowess.

In a nail-biting series of matches, Apex's signature entry fragging style shone brightly. His ability to read the game and make split-second decisions was on full display. Each round was a dance of strategy and reflexes, with Apex leading the charge, securing crucial kills that turned the tide in his team's favor.

As the final round approached, the scoreboard reflected a tense stalemate. It was in this moment that Apex recalled his training, the countless hours of practice, and the support of his teammates. With a deep breath, he executed a daring play that not only eliminated the enemy's star player but also secured the victory for his team.

The roar of the crowd was deafening as they claimed the championship title. This moment was not just a personal triumph for Apex; it was a testament to the hard work, resilience, and camaraderie that defined his journey.

$$\text{Victory} = \text{Teamwork} + \text{Strategy} + \text{Skill} \qquad (30)$$

This formula encapsulates the essence of Apex's success, highlighting that while individual skill is crucial, the synergy within the team is what truly propels a player to greatness.

The Epsilon Era

Following the Intel Championship, Apex's career entered a new phase with his joining of Epsilon Esports. This transition marked a significant turning point, as he was now part of a well-established organization with a rich history in competitive gaming.

Joining Epsilon came with its own set of challenges. Apex was now surrounded by players who were not only skilled but also had their unique playstyles and personalities. Adapting to this new environment required flexibility and open-mindedness. Apex had to learn to navigate team dynamics, balancing his aggressive playstyle with the strategic needs of the team.

$$\text{Adaptation} = \text{Flexibility} + \text{Team Dynamics} \tag{31}$$

Understanding and integrating into the team's strategy became paramount. Apex worked diligently to refine his approach, often experimenting with different roles and tactics during practice sessions. This adaptability proved invaluable as Epsilon began to dominate the global esports scene.

Challenges and Adaptations within the Team

As Epsilon began to rise in the rankings, the pressure to maintain success became a double-edged sword. Apex found himself facing the challenge of sustaining performance under the weight of expectations. The team's success attracted scrutiny, and every match became a test of their resilience.

In response, Apex and his teammates focused on fostering a positive team culture. They implemented regular team-building exercises that encouraged open communication and trust. This camaraderie became essential in navigating the ups and downs of competitive play.

$$\text{Team Success} = \text{Cohesion} + \text{Communication} + \text{Trust} \tag{32}$$

This equation served as a guiding principle for Epsilon, emphasizing that the strength of their relationships off the stage would directly impact their performance on it.

Dominating the Global Esports Scene

Under Apex's leadership and with the synergy of Epsilon, the team began to dominate the global esports scene. Their strategic plays and Apex's entry fragging became the stuff of legends. They racked up victories in several prestigious tournaments, solidifying their reputation as one of the top teams in the world.

Apex's ability to innovate and adapt his playstyle kept opponents guessing. His fearless approach to entry fragging not only secured early advantages for his team but also inspired a new generation of gamers to adopt similar aggressive tactics.

$$\text{Innovation} = \text{Risk-Taking} + \text{Creativity} \qquad (33)$$

This equation highlights the importance of thinking outside the box in competitive gaming, where the ability to surprise opponents can be the key to victory.

Maintaining Success and Winning Streaks

As Epsilon continued to thrive, maintaining success became a focal point for Apex and his teammates. They understood that in the fast-paced world of esports, complacency could lead to downfall.

To counteract this, Apex emphasized the importance of continuous improvement. The team regularly reviewed their gameplay, analyzing matches to identify areas for growth. This commitment to self-reflection and adaptation allowed Epsilon to not only maintain their winning streak but also evolve as a team.

$$\text{Continuous Improvement} = \text{Review} + \text{Adaptation} \qquad (34)$$

This philosophy became ingrained in Epsilon's culture, ensuring that they remained at the forefront of the competitive scene.

In conclusion, Chapter 2: Trials and Triumphs encapsulates the essence of Apex's journey through the Intel Championship and into the Epsilon era. The trials he faced were not mere obstacles but stepping stones that propelled him toward triumph. Each challenge reinforced his resolve, shaping him into the fierce entry fragger he is today. The lessons learned during this period would serve as the foundation for his future endeavors in the ever-evolving landscape of esports.

The Intel Championship

The Journey Towards the Intel Championship

The path to the Intel Championship was not merely a linear ascent; it was a tumultuous journey filled with trials, tribulations, and revelations. For Anjali Esposito, known in the esports realm as Apex, this journey was akin to navigating a labyrinth, fraught with unexpected turns and formidable challenges.

Setting the Stage

In the world of competitive gaming, the Intel Championship stood as a beacon of prestige, attracting the best of the best. The road to this illustrious event began with

Apex's relentless dedication to honing his skills. It was during the early days of his career that he realized the importance of not just individual prowess, but also of team synergy.

The fundamental theory of team dynamics, as described by Tuckman's stages of group development, played a crucial role in shaping the team's trajectory. The stages—forming, storming, norming, and performing—were vividly illustrated as Apex and his teammates navigated their way through conflicts and camaraderie. This theory posits that teams must go through a series of phases to achieve optimal performance, and Apex's team was no exception.

Building a Strong Foundation

In the formative months leading to the championship, Apex focused on building a cohesive unit. The initial phase, forming, was characterized by excitement and anticipation, but soon transitioned into storming, where conflicts and power struggles emerged. Apex, as the entry fragger, had to assert his role while ensuring that his teammates felt valued and heard.

Mathematically, one could represent the dynamics of team performance as follows:

$$P = f(E, C, R)$$

where P is the overall performance, E is the individual effort, C is the cohesion among team members, and R represents the role clarity within the team. Apex recognized that maximizing P required a balance between these components.

Overcoming Adversity

As the team prepared for the championship, they faced a series of setbacks. A pivotal moment occurred during a regional qualifier where they were unexpectedly eliminated in the early rounds. This defeat tested their resolve and brought forth the specter of self-doubt. Apex's reaction was a blend of frustration and determination. He understood that adversity often serves as a crucible for greatness.

In psychological terms, this phenomenon aligns with the concept of resilience, which can be defined as the ability to bounce back from setbacks. Research indicates that resilient individuals often possess a growth mindset, viewing challenges as opportunities for learning rather than insurmountable obstacles. Apex adopted this mindset, encouraging his team to reflect on their performance and identify areas for improvement.

Strategizing for Success

With renewed vigor, Apex and his team delved into strategic planning. They analyzed their previous performances using statistical data, identifying key areas for enhancement. The use of metrics such as kill-to-death ratios and objective control percentages became paramount. For example, the team aimed to maintain a kill-to-death ratio of at least 1.5, which they deemed essential for competitive viability.

The strategic framework they employed can be expressed as:

$$S = \sum_{i=1}^{n}(K_i - D_i) \cdot O_i$$

where S is the overall strategy score, K_i represents kills, D_i denotes deaths, and O_i signifies objective contributions for each player i in the team. This mathematical representation allowed them to quantify their strengths and weaknesses, leading to targeted improvements.

The Final Countdown

As the Intel Championship approached, the atmosphere was charged with anticipation. Apex and his team had transformed their initial struggles into a well-oiled machine, ready to face the world's best. The culmination of their efforts was evident in their performance during the final qualifiers, where they showcased remarkable synergy and strategic prowess.

This transformation was not merely technical; it was also psychological. The team had fostered a culture of support and encouragement, essential for maintaining morale under pressure. Apex's ability to lead by example, coupled with his unwavering belief in his team's potential, became a cornerstone of their success.

In conclusion, the journey towards the Intel Championship was a testament to the power of resilience, teamwork, and strategic foresight. Apex's evolution from a passionate gamer to a formidable competitor was marked by challenges that ultimately forged his identity as a champion. As they stepped onto the grand stage of the Intel Championship, they carried with them not just their skills, but the collective spirit of determination and unity that had defined their journey.

Overcoming Adversity and Mental Roadblocks

In the high-octane world of competitive esports, where the pressure to perform can be as intense as the battles fought in-game, mental resilience becomes not just an asset but a necessity. For Anjali Esposito, known in the gaming realm as Apex, the journey to the pinnacle of esports was fraught with challenges that tested not only his skill but also his mental fortitude.

The Weight of Expectations

As Apex began to rise through the ranks, the expectations placed upon him grew exponentially. The transition from a promising player to a professional athlete is often accompanied by a heavy burden of expectation. This phenomenon can be described through the lens of *performance anxiety*, a psychological condition that affects many athletes. According to the *Yerkes-Dodson Law*, there is an optimal level of arousal for peak performance; however, too much pressure can lead to a decline in performance. Apex found himself navigating this precarious balance, often feeling the weight of not just his ambitions but the aspirations of his fans and teammates.

$$P = \frac{E}{C} \tag{35}$$

where P is performance, E is expectations, and C is coping mechanisms. As expectations increased, without adequate coping strategies, his performance began to waver.

Facing Setbacks

Despite his talent, setbacks were inevitable. During a critical tournament, Apex faced an unexpected defeat against a lower-ranked team. This loss was not just a blow to his career but a significant hit to his self-esteem. The psychological impact of such failures can often lead to a phenomenon known as *impostor syndrome*, where high-achieving individuals doubt their accomplishments and fear being exposed as a "fraud." Apex grappled with these feelings, questioning whether he truly belonged at the top tier of competitive gaming.

Building a Support System

Recognizing the need for support, Apex took proactive steps to address his mental health. He reached out to fellow players, coaches, and mental health professionals. This network became a crucial part of his recovery process. The importance of social support in overcoming mental barriers is well-documented in psychological literature. Research indicates that strong social ties can buffer against the negative effects of stress and enhance resilience.

$$R = S + C \tag{36}$$

where R is resilience, S is social support, and C is coping strategies. Apex learned that by fostering connections with others, he could bolster his resilience against adversity.

Developing Mental Strategies

In addition to building a support network, Apex began to implement mental strategies to combat anxiety and improve focus. Techniques such as visualization, mindfulness, and cognitive restructuring became part of his routine. Visualization, for instance, involves mentally rehearsing scenarios to enhance performance and reduce anxiety. Apex would often visualize himself in high-pressure situations, executing his strategies flawlessly.

Mindfulness, on the other hand, helped him to stay grounded in the present moment, reducing the tendency to ruminate on past failures or future pressures. Research shows that mindfulness can significantly decrease anxiety levels and improve performance in high-stakes environments.

$$M = \frac{A}{F} \tag{37}$$

where M is mindfulness, A is awareness of the present, and F is focus on external distractions. By increasing his mindfulness, Apex was able to enhance his focus and performance during critical matches.

Embracing Failure as a Teacher

One of the most profound lessons Apex learned was to embrace failure as a teacher rather than a foe. Each setback became an opportunity for growth. This shift in mindset aligns with the concept of *growth mindset*, a term coined by psychologist Carol Dweck. Individuals with a growth mindset view challenges as opportunities to develop their skills rather than insurmountable obstacles.

By reframing his perspective on failure, Apex began to approach challenges with renewed vigor. He understood that every defeat was a stepping stone toward mastery, a lesson that would ultimately serve him well in the fiercely competitive arena of esports.

The Road Ahead

As Apex continued to evolve as a player, he recognized that overcoming adversity and mental roadblocks was not a one-time event but an ongoing journey. The skills he developed and the insights he gained would not only enhance his gameplay but also enrich his life beyond the screen.

In conclusion, the narrative of Anjali Esposito, the fierce entry fragger known as Apex, serves as a testament to the power of resilience in the face of adversity. Through the challenges he faced, he not only emerged as a formidable competitor but also as a beacon of hope for aspiring gamers navigating their paths in the often tumultuous world of esports. His story reminds us that while the road to success may be riddled with obstacles, it is also paved with opportunities for growth, learning, and ultimately, triumph.

The Unforgettable Victory

In the grand tapestry of esports, few moments shine as brightly as the unforgettable victory that Anjali Esposito, known in the gaming realm as Apex, achieved during the Intel Championship. This moment was not merely a culmination of skill and strategy; it was a testament to the resilience of the human spirit when faced with insurmountable odds.

The Build-Up to the Championship

Leading up to the Intel Championship, Apex and his team faced a series of challenges that tested their resolve. The rigorous training regimen, filled with hours of practice, strategy discussions, and team-building exercises, was a double-edged sword. The pressure to perform weighed heavily on their shoulders. As the tournament approached, the stakes were higher than ever, and the doubts began to creep in.

The team had been preparing for months, focusing on refining their strategies and understanding their opponents' weaknesses. They meticulously analyzed past matches, creating a database of strategies that could be employed during critical moments. The formula for victory was not just about individual skill, but about teamwork, communication, and the ability to adapt in real-time.

The Day of Reckoning

On the day of the championship, the atmosphere was electric. The venue buzzed with excitement as fans filled the stands, their cheers echoing like a thunderstorm.

Apex, feeling the weight of expectation, took a deep breath, reminding himself of the countless hours spent training and the sacrifices made along the way.

As the match commenced, Apex showcased his signature playstyle—aggressive yet calculated. His ability to read the game and anticipate enemy movements was unmatched. The first few rounds were a rollercoaster of emotions, with both teams trading blows like heavyweight boxers. Apex's team was behind, struggling to find their footing, but he remained resolute.

The Turning Point

The turning point came during a pivotal round where Apex executed a daring maneuver that would later be etched into the annals of esports history. With his team on the brink of elimination, he made the audacious decision to flank the enemy team. This strategic gamble was rooted in the principles of game theory, particularly the Nash Equilibrium, which suggests that in a competitive situation, players can benefit from unpredictable strategies.

Apex's calculated risk paid off. He eliminated two opponents in quick succession, shifting the momentum in favor of his team. The crowd erupted in a cacophony of cheers, and the energy in the arena surged. It was a moment of sheer brilliance, a reminder that sometimes, fortune favors the bold.

Seizing the Moment

With newfound confidence, Apex and his team rallied. They executed their strategies with precision, working in unison as if they were an orchestra playing a symphony. Each player knew their role, and their synergy was palpable. The synergy can be modeled as follows:

$$S = \sum_{i=1}^{n} P_i$$

where S represents the overall synergy, P_i represents the performance of each individual player, and n is the number of players. As performance levels rose, so did the team's morale, and they began to dismantle their opponents with a series of flawless plays.

The Climactic Finale

As the final round approached, the tension in the air was thick enough to cut with a knife. Apex, now fully in the zone, channeled the energy of the crowd into his gameplay. He executed a flawless series of headshots, showcasing not only his mechanical skill but also his mental fortitude. The final moments of the match were a blur, with Apex leading the charge, his heart pounding in rhythm with the frantic clicks of his mouse.

When the last opponent fell, and the victory screen flashed before their eyes, a wave of euphoria washed over the team. They had not only won the championship but had done so against all odds. The unforgettable victory was not just a personal achievement for Apex but a collective triumph that solidified their legacy in the esports world.

The Aftermath

In the aftermath of the victory, Apex became a household name. Interviews flooded in, and fans clamored for a glimpse of the player who had defied expectations. The victory at the Intel Championship was a watershed moment, not only for Apex but for the entire esports community. It inspired countless aspiring gamers, proving that with determination, skill, and a little bit of audacity, greatness is within reach.

The lessons learned during this unforgettable victory extend beyond the gaming arena. They serve as a reminder that resilience, teamwork, and the courage to take risks can lead to extraordinary outcomes. Apex's journey continues to inspire a new generation of gamers, instilling in them the belief that they too can achieve greatness, one game at a time.

Conclusion

In conclusion, the unforgettable victory at the Intel Championship was a defining moment in Apex's career. It encapsulated the essence of competitive gaming—where strategy meets skill, and where the heart of a player shines brightest in the face of adversity. This victory not only marked a significant milestone in Apex's journey but also set the stage for the future of esports, proving that legends are born in the heat of battle.

The Epsilon Era

Joining Epsilon Esports

In the ever-evolving world of competitive gaming, the transition from a promising player to a recognized professional is often fraught with challenges and opportunities. For Anjali Esposito, known in the gaming realm as Apex, joining

Epsilon Esports marked a pivotal moment in her career, serving as both a launching pad and a crucible of growth.

The allure of Epsilon Esports was undeniable. Established as one of the premier organizations in the esports domain, Epsilon boasted a roster of seasoned players and a reputation for fostering talent. However, this opportunity came with its own set of challenges, as Anjali would soon discover.

The Decision to Join

The decision to join Epsilon was not made lightly. Anjali weighed her options carefully, considering the implications of joining a team with such high expectations. Theoretical frameworks in decision-making, such as the Rational Choice Theory, suggest that individuals make decisions by evaluating the potential benefits against the costs. In Anjali's case, the potential benefits included access to advanced training resources, a supportive community, and the chance to compete at higher levels. However, the costs were equally significant, involving the pressure to perform and the risk of public scrutiny.

$$U = B - C \qquad (38)$$

Where U is the utility of the decision, B represents the benefits, and C denotes the costs. In Anjali's mind, the equation balanced favorably, leading her to commit to Epsilon Esports.

Initial Challenges

Upon joining Epsilon, Anjali faced the initial challenge of integrating into an established team. Each member brought unique strengths and weaknesses, and the dynamics of team synergy were crucial. A study on team dynamics in esports highlights that successful teams often exhibit a high level of communication and trust among members [?].

Anjali quickly learned that her role as an entry fragger required not only individual skill but also an acute awareness of team strategies. The concept of role specialization in esports emphasizes that players must understand their responsibilities within the team framework to maximize effectiveness. This was particularly true for Anjali, whose aggressive playstyle needed to be harmonized with her teammates' tactics.

Developing Team Chemistry

Building chemistry with her new teammates was essential. Anjali participated in numerous scrimmages, where the focus was not just on individual performance but on fostering a cohesive unit. Research indicates that teams with strong interpersonal relationships tend to perform better under pressure [?].

Anjali embraced this philosophy, often staying late after practice to review game footage and discuss strategies with her teammates. This dedication to team cohesion paid off as they began to develop a shared understanding of each other's playstyles, allowing for more fluid and effective gameplay.

Overcoming Adversity

However, the journey was not without its hurdles. As Epsilon began to compete in various tournaments, Anjali faced the pressure of expectations. The esports community is known for its intense scrutiny, and players often deal with criticism from fans and analysts alike. Anjali, while resilient, found herself grappling with self-doubt during a particularly challenging tournament where the team failed to meet their goals.

To combat these feelings, Anjali turned to mental health strategies, including mindfulness and visualization techniques. The importance of mental wellness in esports cannot be overstated; research shows that mental resilience is a key factor in maintaining peak performance [?].

The Turning Point

The turning point came during a regional qualifier where Epsilon faced off against a rival team. Anjali's performance was stellar, showcasing her skill as an entry fragger. She led the charge in several rounds, demonstrating not only her technical prowess but also her ability to inspire her teammates.

This match served as a catalyst for the team's success, solidifying their reputation in the esports community. The victory was not just a win on the scoreboard; it represented the culmination of hard work, team chemistry, and Anjali's determination to prove herself as a formidable player.

Conclusion

Joining Epsilon Esports was a transformative experience for Anjali Esposito. It was a journey marked by challenges, growth, and ultimately, triumph. As she navigated the complexities of team dynamics and the pressures of competition, Anjali emerged not just as a player but as a symbol of resilience in the esports landscape. This chapter of her life laid the groundwork for future successes and established her as a key figure in the realm of competitive gaming.

Challenges and Adaptations within the Team

Joining Epsilon Esports marked a pivotal moment in Apex's career, but it was not without its fair share of challenges. The transition from a relatively unknown player to a recognized member of a prominent team came with heightened expectations, both from the organization and from the fans. This section explores the multifaceted challenges faced by Apex and the adaptations that were necessary to thrive in the competitive environment of Epsilon Esports.

Navigating Team Dynamics

One of the most significant challenges Apex encountered was navigating the intricate dynamics of a well-established team. Epsilon was not just any team; it was a powerhouse in the esports arena, boasting a roster filled with seasoned veterans. The existing members had their established roles, strategies, and chemistry, which meant that Apex had to find his place without disrupting the balance.

$$\text{Team Cohesion} = \frac{\text{Individual Contributions}}{\text{Team Conflicts}} \tag{39}$$

The equation above illustrates the delicate balance of team cohesion, where individual contributions must outweigh any potential conflicts. Apex quickly learned that communication was vital. He began to hold one-on-one discussions with teammates to understand their playstyles and preferences, fostering an environment of openness and collaboration. This adaptation not only helped him integrate but also contributed to a more harmonious team atmosphere.

Adapting to Different Playstyles

Epsilon's existing strategies were deeply ingrained, and Apex had to adapt his playstyle to fit the team's needs. Initially, his aggressive entry fragging approach clashed with the more calculated strategies favored by his teammates. This led to a few early miscommunications during scrims and tournaments, resulting in unfavorable outcomes.

To address this, Apex engaged in extensive analysis of past games, both his own and those of his teammates. By dissecting gameplay footage, he identified key moments where his aggression could be tempered with strategic restraint. This adaptation is exemplified in the following equation, which models the relationship between aggression and strategic execution:

$$\text{Success Rate} = \frac{\text{Aggression} \times \text{Strategy}}{\text{Risk}} \qquad (40)$$

Through this lens, Apex learned to balance his natural instincts with the strategic needs of the team, leading to improved synergy and performance.

Overcoming Internal Conflicts

Despite the initial successes, internal conflicts began to arise as the pressure mounted. Differences in opinion regarding strategies and roles led to tension within the squad. Apex found himself in the middle of these disagreements, often feeling the weight of mediating discussions between teammates.

To overcome this, Apex championed a series of team-building exercises, both online and offline. These included strategy workshops, where each member could present their ideas and concerns in a constructive manner. By fostering an environment where everyone felt heard, Apex helped to diffuse tensions and re-establish trust among teammates.

$$\text{Team Trust} = \frac{\text{Open Communication} + \text{Mutual Respect}}{\text{Conflict}} \qquad (41)$$

This equation highlights the importance of trust in team dynamics. As communication improved and respect was cultivated, the conflicts that once threatened to derail the team began to diminish, allowing Epsilon to refocus on their shared goals.

Embracing Change and Growth

The esports landscape is ever-evolving, and teams must adapt to remain competitive. Apex recognized that the only constant in this industry was change. As new strategies emerged and rival teams adapted, Epsilon had to stay ahead of the curve. This required a shift in mindset, where players had to be willing to embrace change rather than resist it.

To facilitate this, Apex took the initiative to encourage a culture of continuous learning within the team. He advocated for regular review sessions, where the team would analyze not just their own gameplay but also that of their competitors. This proactive approach to learning allowed Epsilon to remain adaptable and responsive to the shifting dynamics of the competitive scene.

$$\text{Adaptability} = \frac{\text{Willingness to Learn}}{\text{Resistance to Change}} \quad (42)$$

This equation encapsulates the essence of adaptability in esports. By fostering a willingness to learn and minimizing resistance to change, Epsilon positioned itself as a formidable force in the competitive arena.

Conclusion

The challenges Apex faced within Epsilon Esports were manifold, ranging from navigating team dynamics to overcoming internal conflicts. However, through effective communication, strategic adaptation, and a commitment to continuous growth, he not only found his place within the team but also contributed to its evolution as a leading force in the esports world. This journey of adaptation and resilience not only solidified Apex's reputation as a top fragger but also laid the groundwork for the incredible successes that followed in the years to come.

Dominating the Global Esports Scene

As the sun set over the digital battlegrounds, a new dawn was breaking for Anjali Esposito, better known by her gamer tag, Apex. With her fierce entry-fragging skills and an uncanny ability to read the game like a seasoned maestro, she was not just playing; she was composing a symphony of dominance in the global esports arena. This section delves into the intricacies of her rise, exploring the strategies, mental fortitude, and the sheer will that propelled her into the limelight.

The Strategy Behind Success

To understand how Apex dominated the global esports scene, one must first appreciate the strategic underpinnings of her gameplay. At the core of her success was a meticulous approach to developing a signature playstyle that was both aggressive and calculated. The following equation encapsulates the essence of her gameplay strategy:

$$\text{Success} = \frac{\text{Skill} \times \text{Strategy}}{\text{Risk}} \quad (43)$$

Where: - **Skill** represents Apex's mechanical prowess and game sense. - **Strategy** embodies her tactical approach to each match. - **Risk** signifies the calculated risks taken during gameplay.

Apex's ability to balance these elements allowed her to maximize her impact in matches while minimizing unnecessary losses. For instance, during the Intel Championship, she executed a daring flanking maneuver that caught her opponents off guard, leading to a critical victory that showcased her strategic acumen.

Mental Resilience and Adaptation

In the high-stakes world of esports, mental resilience is as crucial as technical skill. Apex's journey was fraught with challenges that tested her psychological fortitude. The pressure to perform at an elite level can lead to anxiety and self-doubt, especially when representing a prominent team on the international stage.

To combat these mental hurdles, Apex adopted a multifaceted approach to mental wellness. She engaged in mindfulness practices, such as meditation and visualization techniques, which have been shown to enhance focus and reduce anxiety. Research indicates that athletes who incorporate mental training into their routine often experience improved performance outcomes (Vealey, 2007). Apex's ability to remain composed under pressure became a hallmark of her gameplay, enabling her to make split-second decisions that often turned the tide of battle.

The Role of Team Dynamics

Apex's success was not solely attributable to her individual skills; it was also a product of effective team dynamics. The synergy between team members is a critical factor in esports, where communication and collaboration can make or break a match. Apex thrived in an environment that emphasized teamwork, where each player understood their role and could adapt to the evolving dynamics of the game.

The concept of *collective efficacy*—the shared belief in the team's ability to succeed—played a significant role in their victories. Bandura (1997) posits that collective efficacy can enhance performance by fostering motivation and resilience. Apex's team, Epsilon Esports, exemplified this principle as they trained rigorously, developing strategies that leveraged each player's strengths while addressing weaknesses.

Examples of Dominance

Apex's rise to prominence was punctuated by several key victories that solidified her status in the esports community. One notable example was the championship match against Team Pinnacle, where Apex's performance was nothing short of legendary.

With a combination of precise aim and strategic positioning, she secured a staggering 18 eliminations in a single match, leading her team to a resounding victory.

Another critical moment came during the global finals of the Epsilon Era. Faced with a formidable opponent, Apex's ability to adapt her strategy on the fly proved invaluable. When her team found themselves in a precarious situation, she initiated a bold play that turned the match in their favor, showcasing her innate understanding of the game's mechanics and her teammates' capabilities.

Challenges and Overcoming Adversity

Despite her meteoric rise, the path to dominance was not without its challenges. The esports landscape is rife with fierce competition, and maintaining a top position requires constant adaptation and innovation. Apex faced numerous obstacles, including injuries, burnout, and the ever-present threat of emerging talent.

One of the most significant challenges came during a particularly grueling tournament season, where the pressure to perform led to a temporary decline in her gameplay. This period of adversity tested her resolve, but it also served as a catalyst for growth. By reevaluating her training regimen and seeking mentorship from seasoned players, Apex was able to regain her form and emerge even stronger.

Conclusion

In conclusion, Apex's journey to dominating the global esports scene is a testament to her skill, strategic mindset, and resilience. Through a combination of meticulous planning, mental fortitude, and effective teamwork, she carved out her place among the legends of esports. Her story serves as an inspiration to aspiring gamers worldwide, illustrating that with dedication and the right mindset, dominance in the esports arena is within reach.

As the digital curtain falls on this chapter of Apex's career, one thing remains clear: she is not just a player; she is a force to be reckoned with in the world of competitive gaming.

Maintaining Success and Winning Streaks

In the high-octane world of esports, maintaining success and achieving winning streaks is akin to walking a tightrope suspended over a chasm of expectations, rivalries, and the ever-looming specter of burnout. For Anjali Esposito, known in the gaming realm as Apex, this challenge was not merely a matter of skill but a complex interplay of strategy, psychology, and team dynamics.

The Psychological Edge

To delve into the essence of maintaining success, one must first understand the psychological factors at play. Winning streaks can create a phenomenon known as the "winner's effect," where the confidence gained from successive victories can enhance performance in subsequent matches. This is often framed within the context of the following equation:

$$P_{success} = f(C, E, S) \qquad (44)$$

where:

- $P_{success}$ is the probability of winning,
- C represents confidence levels,
- E denotes team synergy and communication,
- S signifies strategic execution.

As Apex's team continued to secure victories, their confidence soared, leading to a self-reinforcing cycle of success. However, this psychological edge is a double-edged sword; the pressure to maintain performance can lead to anxiety and fear of failure. Apex navigated this delicate balance by fostering an environment where open communication and mental wellness were prioritized, allowing players to express concerns and share strategies without fear of judgment.

Team Dynamics and Synergy

The importance of team dynamics cannot be overstated in the pursuit of sustained success. Apex's rise coincided with his ability to cultivate a cohesive unit, where each player understood their role and responsibilities. This synergy is often encapsulated in Tuckman's stages of group development: forming, storming, norming, and performing. Apex's team exemplified the performing stage, where collaboration and trust enabled them to execute complex strategies seamlessly.

For instance, during a pivotal tournament, Apex and his teammates employed a strategy known as "crossfire," where players positioned themselves to cover each other's vulnerabilities. This tactic not only showcased their individual skills but also highlighted their collective understanding of the game, leading to a string of victories that reinforced their reputation as a dominant force in the esports arena.

Adapting to the Meta

Esports is an ever-evolving landscape, with game mechanics and player strategies shifting as frequently as the tides. Maintaining success requires a keen awareness of the current meta—an amalgamation of strategies, character strengths, and player trends that define competitive play. Apex's ability to adapt to these changes was instrumental in his team's sustained success.

Consider the case of the "Apex Meta Shift" during a major championship. As new characters were introduced, and existing ones were rebalanced, Apex's team quickly analyzed the implications of these changes. They conducted rigorous practice sessions, experimenting with different character combinations and strategies, allowing them to stay ahead of their competitors. This adaptability is encapsulated in the following model:

$$M_{adapt} = \frac{R_{new}}{R_{old}} \times T \tag{45}$$

where:

- M_{adapt} is the measure of adaptability,
- R_{new} represents the effectiveness of new strategies,
- R_{old} denotes the effectiveness of previous strategies,
- T signifies the time invested in practice and analysis.

By continuously refining their approach, Apex's team not only maintained their winning streak but also set trends that other teams would strive to emulate.

The Role of Preparation and Analysis

Preparation is the bedrock upon which success is built. Apex and his team dedicated countless hours to analyzing gameplay footage, studying opponents, and rehearsing strategies. This level of preparation is often quantified through the concept of "game hours," where the correlation between practice time and performance is established:

$$G = \alpha \cdot H + \beta \tag{46}$$

where:

- G is the game performance,
- H is the number of hours practiced,

- α and β are constants that reflect the diminishing returns of practice over time.

Apex's relentless commitment to preparation ensured that when the pressure mounted, they were not merely reacting to the game but executing a well-rehearsed plan.

Examples of Winning Streaks

Apex's career is dotted with examples of remarkable winning streaks that not only solidified his status as a top player but also left an indelible mark on the esports community. One such instance occurred during the Intel Championship, where Apex's team achieved an unprecedented series of victories, culminating in a thrilling final match that showcased their strategic prowess and psychological resilience.

During this championship, Apex's team faced a formidable rival, Team Pinnacle, known for their aggressive playstyle. By leveraging their winning momentum and employing adaptive strategies, they managed to outmaneuver their opponents, securing victory after victory. This series of wins not only reinforced their confidence but also established a narrative of dominance that would resonate throughout the esports world.

Conclusion

Maintaining success and winning streaks in esports is a multifaceted endeavor that transcends mere skill. It encompasses psychological fortitude, team dynamics, adaptability to the meta, meticulous preparation, and the ability to learn from both victories and defeats. For Apex, these elements coalesced into a formula for success that not only propelled him to the pinnacle of competitive gaming but also inspired a generation of gamers to pursue their dreams with tenacity and passion. As the esports landscape continues to evolve, the lessons learned from Apex's journey will undoubtedly serve as a guiding light for future champions.

The Showdown with Rival Teams

The Intense Rivalry with Team Pinnacle

The rivalry between Apex and Team Pinnacle is a tale woven with threads of fierce competition, strategic brilliance, and unyielding determination. This rivalry not only defined an era in esports but also set a benchmark for what it means to be at the pinnacle of competitive gaming.

A Clash of Titans

The genesis of this rivalry can be traced back to the early days of competitive tournaments where both teams consistently found themselves pitted against each other. Each encounter was not merely a game; it was an epic showdown, a battle of wits and reflexes that drew the attention of fans and analysts alike. The tension was palpable, and the stakes were always high.

$$\text{Rivalry Score} = \frac{\text{Wins}_{Apex} - \text{Wins}_{Pinnacle}}{\text{Total Matches}} \quad (47)$$

This equation illustrates the competitive balance between the two teams. A positive score indicated Apex's dominance, while a negative score favored Pinnacle, reflecting the ebb and flow of victories that characterized their encounters.

Strategic Depth

Both teams employed distinct strategies that showcased their unique playstyles. Apex, known for their aggressive entry fragging, often initiated engagements with high-risk maneuvers designed to disrupt the enemy's formation. In contrast, Team Pinnacle adopted a more calculated approach, focusing on positioning and tactical discipline.

Apex's signature playstyle involved the following elements:

- **Entry Frags:** Apex players, particularly Anjali, would lead the charge, seeking to secure early eliminations to gain a numerical advantage.
- **Map Control:** Controlling key areas of the map was crucial. Apex often utilized smoke grenades and flashbangs to obscure vision and create opportunities for their entry fraggers.
- **Team Coordination:** Communication was vital. Apex's ability to coordinate attacks and call out enemy positions often turned the tide in their favor.

In contrast, Team Pinnacle's strategies included:

- **Defensive Structures:** Pinnacle favored holding positions and utilizing crossfires, making it challenging for Apex to execute their aggressive tactics.
- **Counterplay:** Pinnacle's players were adept at reading Apex's movements, often anticipating their plays and countering effectively.
- **Utility Usage:** Pinnacle's disciplined use of grenades and abilities allowed them to control engagements and minimize Apex's impact.

Memorable Encounters

The rivalry reached its zenith during the Grand Finals of the Intel Championship, where both teams clashed in a best-of-five series that would determine the champion. The atmosphere was electric, with fans from both sides filling the arena, their cheers echoing through the halls.

In the first match, Apex's aggressive strategy paid off, leading to a decisive victory. However, Team Pinnacle adjusted in the second match, showcasing their adaptability and resilience. The series swung back and forth, with each team claiming victories in stunning displays of skill.

The final match was a nail-biter, with both teams trading rounds. Apex's entry fragger, Anjali, delivered a spectacular performance, securing multiple crucial kills. Yet, Pinnacle's composure under pressure allowed them to capitalize on mistakes.

In the end, it was a last-second clutch by Anjali that sealed the victory for Apex, sending the crowd into a frenzy. The series not only solidified Apex's status as a top-tier team but also deepened the rivalry with Team Pinnacle, which would continue to shape the landscape of esports for years to come.

The Aftermath and Legacy

The rivalry with Team Pinnacle left an indelible mark on Apex's legacy. It pushed the team to refine their strategies, enhance their teamwork, and elevate their game to new heights. The intense competition fostered a culture of excellence within Apex, motivating players to strive for greatness.

Moreover, this rivalry became a case study for aspiring teams in the esports community. Analysts often dissected their matches, highlighting the strategic nuances and psychological warfare that unfolded on the virtual battlefield.

As both teams continued to compete at the highest levels, their rivalry evolved into a mutual respect. Apex and Team Pinnacle recognized that their battles had not only shaped their careers but had also contributed to the growth of esports as a legitimate sport.

In conclusion, the intense rivalry with Team Pinnacle was more than just a series of matches; it was a defining chapter in the story of Apex. It showcased the beauty of competitive gaming, where skill, strategy, and passion collide in a spectacular display of talent. The echoes of their encounters resonate through the annals of esports history, serving as a testament to the spirit of competition that drives athletes to push their limits and redefine what is possible.

Apex vs. Nemesis: Clash of Titans

The rivalry between Apex and Nemesis is often heralded as one of the most electrifying narratives in the annals of esports history. This chapter unfolds the saga of two formidable teams, each vying for supremacy in the competitive gaming arena, and how their confrontations shaped the landscape of esports.

The Build-Up to the Rivalry

The stage was set in the early days of the international esports circuit, where Apex, known for their aggressive entry fragging and tactical prowess, emerged as a formidable force. On the other side stood Nemesis, a team characterized by their strategic depth and disciplined gameplay. The two teams clashed repeatedly in various tournaments, each encounter intensifying the rivalry and elevating the stakes.

Analyzing Team Dynamics

In the world of competitive gaming, team dynamics play a crucial role in determining outcomes. Apex's playstyle was rooted in high-risk, high-reward strategies, often relying on the individual skill of their entry fraggers to secure early kills. The equation governing their success can be summarized as follows:

$$\text{Success}_{Apex} = \text{Skill}_{Entry} + \text{Team Coordination} + \text{Adaptability} \quad (48)$$

Whereas Nemesis adopted a more calculated approach, focusing on positioning and map control. Their formula for success could be expressed as:

$$\text{Success}_{Nemesis} = \text{Tactical Execution} + \text{Communication} + \text{Resource Management} \quad (49)$$

The juxtaposition of these two philosophies created a captivating spectacle, drawing in fans and analysts alike.

Epic Encounters

One of the most memorable encounters occurred during the Grand Finals of the Intel Championship. The atmosphere was electric, with fans from both sides filling the arena, their chants echoing through the halls. The match was a rollercoaster of emotions, showcasing the strengths and weaknesses of both teams.

In Game 1, Apex took an early lead, leveraging their aggressive style to dominate the map. However, Nemesis quickly adapted, countering with strategic plays that turned the tide in their favor. This back-and-forth battle exemplified the essence of competition, where adaptability and resilience were tested to the limits.

The pivotal moment came during the final round of Game 5, where Apex's entry fragger, known by the moniker "Apex Predator," executed a flawless flank maneuver that secured a critical victory. The crowd erupted, and the moment became etched in the lore of esports, symbolizing the raw intensity of the rivalry.

Theoretical Implications

From a theoretical perspective, the Apex vs. Nemesis rivalry illustrates the concepts of game theory and competitive strategy. Each team was not only competing against each other but also engaging in a psychological battle, anticipating the other's moves and adapting their strategies accordingly. This dynamic can be analyzed through the lens of Nash Equilibrium, where each team's strategy is optimal given the strategy of the other.

$$\text{Nash Equilibrium:} \quad \forall i, \quad \text{Strategy}_i \in \{\text{Best Response to Strategy}_{-i}\} \quad (50)$$

In simpler terms, each team aimed to maximize their chances of winning while minimizing the potential for defeat, leading to a series of mind games that captivated audiences and analysts.

Cultural Impact

The rivalry transcended the confines of the gaming arena, influencing popular culture and inspiring a new generation of gamers. Apex's audacious style and Nemesis's tactical genius became archetypes for aspiring players, shaping their understanding of competitive play. Merchandise, fan art, and social media discussions proliferated, creating a cultural phenomenon that extended beyond the games themselves.

Conclusion

The clashes between Apex and Nemesis were more than mere matches; they were epic narratives woven into the fabric of esports history. Each encounter not only showcased the skill and determination of the players but also highlighted the evolution of competitive gaming as a legitimate sport. As the dust settled on their rivalry, one thing remained clear: the legacy of Apex and Nemesis would continue to inspire future generations, reminding them of the passion, perseverance, and thrill that defines the world of esports.

The Never-Ending Battle for Supremacy

In the electrifying world of esports, the quest for supremacy is not merely a series of matches; it is a relentless battle that tests the mettle of athletes, teams, and their strategies. For Anjali Esposito, known in the competitive arena as Apex, this struggle became a defining aspect of his career, particularly during his confrontations with rival teams that sought to dethrone him and his squad.

The Stakes of Competition

The esports landscape is characterized by its fierce competitiveness, where each match can pivot the trajectory of a player's career. In this high-stakes environment, the desire for dominance fuels rivalries, often leading to intense showdowns that capture the attention of fans worldwide. Apex's encounters with Team Pinnacle and Nemesis exemplified this phenomenon, where every victory and defeat carried significant implications not only for rankings but also for personal pride and legacy.

Strategic Depth and Adaptation

The essence of the battle for supremacy lies in the strategic depth that teams must navigate. Apex and his team developed a playstyle that emphasized aggression and precision, a hallmark of their identity. This approach necessitated continuous adaptation, as rival teams analyzed and countered their tactics. The mathematical framework of game theory provides insight into this dynamic, where players must anticipate opponents' moves while optimizing their own strategies.

Let S represent a strategy set, and let P denote the payoff matrix reflecting the outcomes of various strategies against one another. The equilibrium of such a game can be expressed as:

$$\max_{s_i \in S} \sum_{j \neq i} P_{ij}(s_i, s_j)$$

where s_i is the strategy chosen by Apex's team and s_j represents the strategies of rival teams. This equation captures the essence of competitive strategy: maximizing one's payoff while considering the responses of opponents.

THE SHOWDOWN WITH RIVAL TEAMS

The Rivalry with Team Pinnacle

The rivalry with Team Pinnacle was particularly intense, marked by a series of high-stakes matches that drew in massive audiences. Each encounter was a spectacle, with both teams vying for dominance. Pinnacle's strategy often involved a more defensive approach, contrasting with Apex's aggressive style. The clash of these philosophies led to thrilling matches where tactical execution and psychological warfare played pivotal roles.

For instance, during the championship finals, Apex's team adopted a novel strategy, dubbed "The Blitz," which involved rapid, coordinated attacks aimed at dismantling Pinnacle's defenses. The success of this strategy can be analyzed through the lens of Nash Equilibrium, where the optimal response to an opponent's strategy is crucial. Apex's ability to innovate under pressure showcased his prowess as a top fragger and a strategic mastermind.

The Clash with Nemesis

The rivalry with Nemesis represented another chapter in the saga of competitive supremacy. This team, known for its exceptional teamwork and synergy, posed a unique challenge to Apex and his squad. The psychological aspects of this rivalry were palpable; each match was not just about skill but also about mental fortitude. Apex's team had to overcome not only the tactical challenges posed by Nemesis but also the pressure of expectations from fans and sponsors.

In a critical match, Apex found himself facing a seemingly insurmountable deficit. The team was down by several rounds, and the pressure mounted. It was during this moment that Apex's leadership shone. He rallied his teammates, employing a strategy that emphasized communication and trust. The mathematical concept of resilience in game theory comes into play here, where the ability to bounce back from setbacks is crucial for maintaining competitive edge.

The Aftermath and Legacy of Rivalries

The battles against Pinnacle and Nemesis left an indelible mark on Apex's career and the esports community. These rivalries not only shaped the trajectory of his professional journey but also influenced the evolution of team strategies within the industry. Apex's innovative approaches to gameplay and his ability to adapt under pressure became benchmarks for aspiring esports athletes.

The legacy of these encounters extends beyond mere statistics; they serve as a testament to the spirit of competition in esports. Each match was a narrative of struggle, resilience, and triumph, encapsulating the essence of what it means to be a competitor in this dynamic field. As Apex continued to rise through the ranks, his battles against these formidable rivals became legendary, inspiring a new generation of gamers to embrace the thrill of competition and the pursuit of excellence.

In conclusion, the never-ending battle for supremacy in esports is a multifaceted journey that intertwines strategy, psychology, and personal growth. For Apex, these rivalries were not just obstacles to overcome but defining moments that shaped his identity as a player and a cultural icon in the gaming world. The echoes of these battles resonate within the community, reminding us all of the relentless pursuit of greatness that defines the spirit of esports.

A Legacy in the Making

Apex's Impact on Team Strategy and Dynamics

Apex, known for his aggressive entry fragging style, has not only carved a niche for himself in the esports realm but has also significantly influenced team strategies and dynamics within the competitive landscape. His approach to gameplay has inspired a paradigm shift in how teams structure their tactics, emphasizing the importance of synergy, communication, and adaptability.

The Role of Entry Fragging

Entry fragging is a critical role in team-based shooters, where the player is tasked with initiating engagements and creating openings for their teammates. Apex's unique ability to secure early kills while gathering crucial information has redefined the expectations of this role. The equation for success in entry fragging can be simplified to:

$$\text{Team Success} = \text{Entry Fragger's Kills} + \text{Information Gathered} + \text{Team Coordination} \tag{51}$$

This equation illustrates that while individual performance is vital, the interplay between kills, information, and teamwork is what ultimately leads to victory.

Innovative Strategies

Apex's gameplay has led to the development of innovative strategies that prioritize aggressive map control. His ability to read opponents and adapt to their movements has encouraged teams to adopt a more proactive approach. For example, during a crucial match against Team Pinnacle, Apex's early aggression forced the opposing team to play defensively, allowing his team to dictate the pace of the game. This strategy of leveraging early aggression to control the tempo has become a staple for many teams following his lead.

Synergy and Communication

One of Apex's most significant contributions to team dynamics is the emphasis on synergy and communication. His gameplay relies heavily on the seamless coordination between teammates. Apex often utilizes voice comms to relay critical information, such as enemy positions and potential threats. This focus on communication has led to a more structured approach within teams, where players are encouraged to share information actively, fostering a culture of collaboration.

Apex's influence can be seen in the implementation of structured communication protocols, where teams establish specific callouts and signals to enhance in-game coordination. For instance, during the Intel Championship, Apex's team utilized a system where players would call out their intentions before engagements, leading to a notable increase in their win rate.

Adapting to Meta Shifts

The esports landscape is ever-evolving, with new metas emerging as games are updated and players innovate. Apex's adaptability has set an example for teams to remain flexible in their strategies. He has shown that understanding the meta is crucial but that true mastery lies in the ability to adapt strategies on the fly.

For instance, when a new weapon was introduced in a popular title, Apex quickly integrated it into his playstyle, demonstrating its potential in entry fragging scenarios. This adaptability not only helped his team stay ahead of the competition but also encouraged other players to experiment with new tactics, leading to a broader evolution of strategies across the esports scene.

Challenges and Counter Strategies

While Apex's impact on team strategy has been profound, it has not been without challenges. As his playstyle gained recognition, rival teams began to develop counter-strategies specifically aimed at neutralizing his effectiveness. This arms race of tactics necessitated that Apex and his team continuously evolve their strategies to maintain their competitive edge.

For example, after facing a series of losses against teams that effectively countered his aggressive entry, Apex and his team conducted extensive reviews of their gameplay. They identified patterns in their strategies that opponents exploited and adjusted their approach accordingly. This iterative process of learning and adaptation underscores the dynamic nature of esports and the necessity for teams to remain vigilant and responsive.

Conclusion

In summary, Apex's impact on team strategy and dynamics is a testament to his skill and understanding of competitive gaming. His aggressive entry fragging style has not only reshaped how teams approach engagements but has also fostered a culture of communication, synergy, and adaptability. As the esports landscape continues to evolve, Apex's influence will undoubtedly leave a lasting legacy, inspiring future generations of gamers to innovate and collaborate in their pursuit of excellence.

Bibliography

[1] Smith, J. (2021). *The Art of Entry Fragging: Strategies for Success.* Esports Journal, 15(3), 45-60.

[2] Johnson, L. (2022). *Team Dynamics in Esports: Communication and Coordination.* Gaming Psychology Review, 12(1), 22-34.

[3] Williams, R. (2023). *Adapting to Change: The Evolution of Esports Strategies.* Competitive Gaming Journal, 8(2), 78-90.

Pioneering New Techniques and Strategies

In the ever-evolving landscape of competitive esports, the ability to innovate and adapt is paramount. Anjali Esposito, known in the gaming world as Apex, has not only embraced this ethos but has also become a beacon of strategic ingenuity. Through a combination of analytical prowess, instinctual gameplay, and a deep understanding of team dynamics, Apex has pioneered new techniques and strategies that have redefined the role of an entry fragger.

The Concept of Entry Fragging

At its core, entry fragging is the art of being the first player to engage the enemy team, often at the cost of one's own life. The entry fragger's primary objective is to create space for their teammates by either securing the first kill or forcing the opposing team into a defensive posture. Apex's approach to entry fragging is rooted in the principles of game theory, where the decisions made by players can be analyzed through the lens of strategic interaction.

$$U_i = \sum_{j \neq i} p_{ij} \cdot v_{ij} \qquad (52)$$

In this equation, U_i represents the utility of player i, p_{ij} denotes the probability of player i successfully eliminating player j, and v_{ij} is the value gained from that elimination. Apex's ability to maximize U_i through calculated risks has set him apart in the competitive scene.

Innovative Techniques

Apex's innovative techniques can be categorized into several key strategies:

- **Dynamic Entry Techniques:** Apex has developed a method of entry that combines unpredictability with precision. By utilizing a mix of utility grenades, such as smoke and flashbangs, he creates opportunities for his team to capitalize on disoriented opponents. This technique often involves a calculated risk assessment, weighing the potential gain against the likelihood of failure.

- **Information Gathering:** Apex emphasizes the importance of information in gameplay. His strategy includes taking on the role of a scout, using sound cues and map knowledge to relay critical information to his teammates. This proactive approach allows his team to make informed decisions, often leading to advantageous engagements.

- **Adaptive Playstyle:** The ability to adapt to the opposing team's strategies is crucial. Apex has demonstrated a remarkable skill in reading the game, adjusting his playstyle based on the enemy's movements and tactics. This adaptability not only enhances his effectiveness as an entry fragger but also elevates the overall performance of his team.

- **Psychological Warfare:** Apex understands that esports is as much a mental game as it is a physical one. By employing mind games, such as fakes and feints, he can manipulate the enemy's positioning and decision-making. This psychological aspect of gameplay is often overlooked but has proven to be a game-changer in high-stakes matches.

Challenges and Solutions

While pioneering new techniques, Apex faced numerous challenges. One significant issue was the resistance from traditionalists within the esports community who favored established strategies. To address this, Apex focused on demonstrating the effectiveness of his techniques through consistent results in tournaments. By leading his team to victory using these innovative strategies, he gradually gained acceptance and respect from peers and critics alike.

Another challenge was the need for seamless communication within the team. Apex recognized that even the most brilliant strategy could falter without proper coordination. To overcome this, he initiated regular team meetings and practice sessions, fostering an environment where open dialogue and constructive feedback were encouraged. This approach not only improved team synergy but also allowed for the continuous refinement of strategies.

Examples of Success

One of the most notable instances of Apex's pioneering strategies occurred during the finals of the Intel Championship. Faced with a formidable opponent, Apex employed a dynamic entry technique that involved a well-timed smoke grenade followed by a rapid push through a narrow choke point. This maneuver caught the enemy team off-guard, leading to a quick double kill that shifted the momentum of the match.

Another example can be seen during the Epsilon Era, where Apex's adaptive playstyle was put to the test against Team Pinnacle. By meticulously analyzing the enemy's previous matches, he was able to predict their movements and counter their strategies effectively. This foresight allowed Apex and his team to dominate the match, showcasing the power of innovation in competitive gaming.

Legacy of Innovation

Apex's contributions to the field of entry fragging extend beyond his personal achievements. His techniques have inspired a new generation of players to think critically about their roles within a team and to embrace innovation as a fundamental aspect of their gameplay. As esports continues to grow, the strategies pioneered by Apex will undoubtedly leave a lasting impact on the competitive scene, shaping the future of entry fragging and team dynamics.

In conclusion, Anjali Esposito, as Apex, has not only redefined what it means to be an entry fragger but has also set a standard for strategic innovation in esports. Through his pioneering techniques and relentless pursuit of excellence, he has carved out a legacy that will inspire players for years to come.

The Lasting Influence on the Meta

The term *meta* in esports refers to the prevailing strategies, character selections, and gameplay styles that dominate the competitive landscape at any given time. As an entry fragger, Apex's playstyle not only defined his personal approach to the game but also significantly influenced the broader meta within the esports community. This influence can be observed through several key aspects: strategic innovations, character utilization, and the psychological impact on both players and teams.

Strategic Innovations

Apex introduced a unique approach to entry fragging that emphasized aggressive engagement and tactical positioning. Traditionally, entry fraggers would focus solely on securing kills; however, Apex's strategy incorporated an understanding of map control and team dynamics. He often utilized the following equation to illustrate the importance of positioning:

$$\text{Effective Engagement} = \frac{\text{Positioning} \times \text{Team Coordination}}{\text{Risk Factor}} \quad (53)$$

Where:

- **Effective Engagement** refers to the successful initiation of combat.

- **Positioning** denotes the strategic placement of the entry fragger relative to the enemy.

- **Team Coordination** is the level of communication and synergy with teammates.

- **Risk Factor** represents the potential downsides of the chosen approach, such as exposure to enemy fire.

By optimizing this equation, Apex demonstrated that entry fragging could be a calculated risk rather than a reckless endeavor. This shift encouraged other players to adopt similar methodologies, leading to a more strategic and less chaotic approach to entry fragging in competitive matches.

Character Utilization

Apex's choice of characters was also pivotal in reshaping the meta. He favored characters with high mobility and damage output, which allowed him to execute his strategies effectively. For example, his use of characters like *Raze* and *Jett* showcased the importance of agility in securing early kills and controlling the pace of the game. This preference led to a notable increase in the popularity of these characters among other players.

The influence of character selection can be quantified through the *pick rate*, which measures how often a character is chosen in competitive play. As Apex's success grew, the pick rates for his preferred characters surged, illustrating a direct correlation between his gameplay and the evolving meta. The following data exemplifies this trend:

Table 0.1: Character Pick Rates Pre and Post Apex

Character & Pick Rate Pre-Apex & Pick Rate Post-Apex
Raze & 15% & 35%
Jett & 20% & 40%
Sova & 10% & 15%

This data indicates that Apex's gameplay not only popularized certain characters but also shifted the meta towards a more aggressive and fast-paced style, encouraging players to explore high-mobility options.

Psychological Impact

Apex's influence extended beyond mere gameplay mechanics; it also had a profound psychological impact on both opponents and aspiring entry fraggers. His reputation as a formidable entry fragger instilled a sense of fear and respect among rival teams, often forcing them to alter their strategies in anticipation of his aggressive playstyle. This psychological warfare can be described by the following model:

$$\text{Psychological Pressure} = \frac{\text{Reputation} \times \text{Performance}}{\text{Opponent's Confidence}} \qquad (54)$$

Where:

- **Psychological Pressure** reflects the mental burden placed on opponents.
- **Reputation** is the established credibility of the player within the community.
- **Performance** denotes the player's recent successes and skill level.
- **Opponent's Confidence** represents the mental fortitude of rival players.

As Apex continued to dominate the competitive scene, his psychological impact forced teams to rethink their strategies and adapt to his presence, thereby altering the meta dynamics.

Conclusion

In summary, Apex's lasting influence on the meta can be attributed to his strategic innovations, character utilization, and psychological impact on the competitive landscape. By redefining the role of the entry fragger, he not only set new standards for individual performance but also inspired a generation of players to embrace a more strategic approach to gameplay. As the esports community continues to evolve, the legacy of Apex will undoubtedly remain a pivotal chapter in the history of competitive gaming, shaping the meta for years to come.

Trials and Tribulations

Trials and Tribulations

Trials and Tribulations

In the world of competitive esports, the journey is often a rollercoaster, filled with exhilarating highs and devastating lows. For Anjali Esposito, known in the gaming realm as Apex, the trials and tribulations faced during this chapter of his career were not merely challenges; they were defining moments that shaped him into the fierce entry fragger he is today.

The Betrayal

The tale begins with an unexpected twist—betrayal from within his own team. After a series of successful tournaments, the internal dynamics of Apex's team began to shift. Team synergy, once a well-oiled machine, started to show signs of friction. The competitive nature of esports can often lead to tensions that, if not managed properly, can spiral into chaos.

In a shocking turn of events, a key teammate decided to pursue a different path, leading to a fracture in the team's cohesion. This unexpected team split left Apex grappling with feelings of betrayal and confusion. The emotional toll of this event was profound, as trust had been shattered, and the foundation of camaraderie that he had built was now in ruins.

Navigating Team Politics and Personal Conflicts

Navigating the murky waters of team politics became a daunting task. Apex found himself in a position where he had to mediate conflicts, not just for the sake of the team's performance but also for his own mental well-being. The pressure to perform while dealing with personal conflicts created a cacophony of stress.

To illustrate the complexity of team dynamics, consider the following equation that represents the balance of team synergy (S):

$$S = \frac{C + R + T}{N} \tag{55}$$

where: - C is the level of communication, - R is the level of respect among team members, - T is the trust established within the team, - N is the number of team members.

As the values of C, R, and T diminished due to the betrayal, the overall synergy S plummeted, leading to a decrease in performance. This mathematical representation underscores the fragility of team dynamics in esports.

Facing Betrayal with Resilience and Determination

Despite the chaos, Apex chose resilience. Instead of succumbing to despair, he channeled his energy into self-improvement. The experience of betrayal became a catalyst for growth. He sought to understand the psychological aspects of teamwork, delving into literature on conflict resolution and team dynamics.

One pivotal moment was attending a workshop on mental toughness, where he learned to embrace adversity as a stepping stone rather than a stumbling block. Apex began to view challenges as opportunities to refine his skills, both as a player and as a teammate.

The Road to Redemption

With a renewed sense of purpose, Apex made the bold decision to join a new team, Phoenix Rising. This transition was not merely a change of scenery; it was a chance to redefine his identity in the esports arena.

Regaining confidence and form was a journey fraught with challenges. The initial days at Phoenix Rising were marked by a steep learning curve. Apex had to adapt to new strategies and playstyles while earning the trust of his new teammates.

Overcoming Setbacks and Bouncing Back

Setbacks became a familiar companion during this phase. However, with each setback, Apex learned to bounce back stronger. He adopted a mindset that embraced failure as part of the process. The importance of mental resilience became evident, as he frequently reminded himself of the adage: "Fall seven times, stand up eight."

The psychological framework of growth mindset, developed by psychologist Carol Dweck, became a guiding principle for Apex. He learned to cultivate a belief that abilities could be developed through dedication and hard work, which fostered a love for learning and resilience essential for great accomplishments.

The Struggle with Mental Health

While the competitive world of esports often glorifies the triumphs, it seldom highlights the mental health struggles that many athletes face. Apex was no exception. Battling anxiety and depression became part of his narrative. The pressure to perform at an elite level, coupled with the recent betrayal, took a toll on his mental health.

Recognizing the importance of mental wellness, Apex sought professional help. Therapy sessions provided him with tools to manage his anxiety and develop coping strategies. He began to openly discuss mental health within the esports community, advocating for the importance of seeking help.

Rising from the Ashes

In a remarkable turnaround, Apex stepped into the limelight once again. With the support of his new team, he began to experience triumphs and victories that reignited his passion for the game.

The journey with Phoenix Rising was marked by a series of successful tournaments, culminating in a victory that solidified his return to form. This resurgence not only restored his confidence but also proved to critics that he was far from finished.

The narrative of trials and tribulations is not merely a tale of hardship; it is a testament to the resilience of the human spirit. Apex emerged from the shadows of betrayal and despair, stronger and more determined than ever. The road was long and fraught with challenges, yet each trial served as a stepping stone toward greatness.

In conclusion, the trials faced by Apex during this chapter were not just obstacles; they were integral to his evolution as a player and a person. Through resilience, determination, and a commitment to mental wellness, he transformed adversity into a powerful narrative of redemption and triumph.

The Betrayal

The Unexpected Team Split

In the world of esports, where the stakes are as high as the adrenaline rush during a nail-biting match, the bonds formed within a team can be as fragile as the pixels on a screen. For Anjali Esposito, known in the gaming realm as Apex, the unexpected split from his team was not merely a professional setback; it was a seismic shift that reverberated through his career and personal life.

The split occurred during a tumultuous period for the team, which had recently seen a string of impressive victories but was also grappling with internal tensions. The dynamics within the squad had begun to fray, much like a beloved gaming controller that has seen too many intense matches. As the pressure mounted, cracks began to appear in the once-solid foundation of camaraderie.

The Signs of Discord

The first signs of discord were subtle, like the faint hum of a malfunctioning console. Communication, the lifeblood of any successful team, began to falter. Apex noticed that discussions during practice sessions were increasingly laced with tension. The once-constructive critiques morphed into personal attacks, and the playful banter that had fostered a family-like atmosphere turned into silence, punctuated only by the clicking of keyboards.

This shift can be understood through Tuckman's stages of group development, which outline the phases teams typically go through: forming, storming, norming, performing, and adjourning. Apex's team had reached the storming phase, where conflict arises as team members vie for dominance and clarity in roles. The lack of effective conflict resolution strategies exacerbated the situation, leading to misunderstandings and resentment.

The Catalyst for Change

The tipping point came during a critical tournament preparation session. A heated argument erupted between Apex and a fellow teammate regarding strategy. Apex, known for his aggressive entry-fragging style, advocated for a high-risk, high-reward approach, while the teammate favored a more conservative strategy. The disagreement escalated, drawing in other team members and culminating in a public confrontation that left the team fractured.

This incident can be analyzed through the lens of social identity theory, which posits that individuals derive a sense of self from their group memberships. In this case, the clash of identities—Apex as the daring innovator versus his teammate as the cautious strategist—created an environment ripe for division. Each player's perception of their role and importance within the team began to shift, leading to feelings of insecurity and distrust.

The Aftermath

In the wake of the argument, the team attempted to regroup, but the damage was done. The atmosphere was thick with tension, and the once-unbreakable bond between teammates had begun to unravel. Apex found himself at a crossroads, facing the harsh reality that his future with the team was uncertain. The emotional toll was significant; as an athlete who had poured his heart and soul into the team, the prospect of leaving felt akin to losing a part of himself.

The decision to part ways was not solely in Apex's hands. Team management, recognizing the toxicity that had developed, initiated discussions about restructuring the roster. Apex was left to grapple with feelings of betrayal and confusion. The unexpected team split was looming, and the ramifications would extend far beyond the game.

Navigating the Split

As the news of the impending split circulated, the esports community buzzed with speculation. Fans and analysts alike dissected the situation, each offering their own theories about the causes and consequences. The pressure of public scrutiny weighed heavily on Apex, who had always been a figure of inspiration for many aspiring gamers.

In a moment of introspection, Apex realized that he had to take control of his narrative. Drawing on the resilience he had developed over years of competition, he began to focus on personal growth and self-improvement. He sought mentorship from seasoned players and engaged in self-reflection, analyzing not only his gameplay but also his interpersonal skills.

Conclusion

The unexpected team split was a turning point in Apex's career, one that forced him to confront the complexities of team dynamics and personal identity within the esports landscape. While it was a painful chapter, it ultimately set the stage for his next endeavors. The lessons learned during this tumultuous period would become integral to his development as both a player and a leader, shaping his approach to future challenges in the competitive arena.

In the grand tapestry of Apex's journey, the unexpected team split served as a catalyst for transformation, reminding us all that even in the face of adversity, resilience and adaptability can lead to new beginnings.

Navigating Team Politics and Personal Conflicts

In the high-stakes world of esports, where the adrenaline rush of competition meets the intricate web of human relationships, navigating team politics and personal conflicts can often be as challenging as the game itself. For Anjali Esposito, known by his gamer tag Apex, this journey was fraught with tension, misunderstandings, and the relentless pursuit of harmony amidst chaos.

Understanding Team Dynamics

The dynamics of a team can be likened to a complex system where each player's role is interdependent. According to Tuckman's stages of group development, teams typically progress through four stages: forming, storming, norming, and performing. Apex's team initially thrived in the **forming** stage, where excitement and camaraderie flourished. However, as the pressures of competition mounted, they swiftly transitioned into the **storming** stage, characterized by conflicts and power struggles.

$$\text{Team Effectiveness} = \text{Communication} + \text{Trust} + \text{Conflict Resolution} \quad (56)$$

This equation encapsulates the essence of effective teamwork. Communication breaks down when personal conflicts arise, leading to a decline in trust and an inability to resolve differences. Apex found himself at the center of these dynamics, often having to mediate between teammates whose egos clashed like titans on the battlefield.

The Role of Leadership

Leadership plays a pivotal role in mitigating conflicts. In esports, the team captain or coach is tasked with steering the ship through turbulent waters. Apex, despite being a fierce entry fragger, was often called upon to step into a leadership role. He learned that effective leaders employ *transformational leadership* strategies, which inspire and motivate team members to transcend their individual interests for the greater good of the team.

$$\text{Transformational Leadership} = \text{Inspiration} + \text{Intellectual Stimulation} + \text{Individual Consid} \quad (57)$$

Apex realized that by fostering an environment of inspiration and intellectual stimulation, he could help alleviate tensions. He actively encouraged open dialogues during practice sessions, allowing teammates to voice their frustrations and ideas. This approach not only built trust but also cultivated a sense of belonging among team members.

Conflict Resolution Strategies

Navigating personal conflicts requires a toolbox of conflict resolution strategies. Apex adopted several techniques, including:

- **Active Listening:** By genuinely hearing his teammates' concerns, Apex was able to validate their feelings and diffuse tension.

- **Mediation:** When disagreements escalated, he stepped in as a neutral party to facilitate discussions and guide teammates towards a mutual understanding.

- **Setting Boundaries:** Apex emphasized the importance of respecting personal space and boundaries, which helped reduce friction among players with differing personalities.

These strategies proved invaluable during a particularly tumultuous period when two key players were at odds over gameplay strategies. Apex organized a team meeting where each player presented their perspective, fostering a collaborative atmosphere that ultimately led to a consensus on their approach.

Personal Growth and Resilience

Navigating team politics and personal conflicts not only honed Apex's leadership skills but also contributed to his personal growth. He learned to embrace vulnerability, acknowledging his own shortcomings while supporting his teammates through their struggles. This resilience became a cornerstone of his identity, allowing him to emerge stronger from the challenges faced.

In the world of esports, where the line between victory and defeat can be razor-thin, the ability to navigate the intricate dance of team politics is as crucial as mastering the mechanics of the game. Apex's journey through these trials not only shaped his career but also set a precedent for future generations of gamers, illustrating the profound impact of interpersonal relationships in the realm of competitive gaming.

$$\text{Resilience} = \text{Growth Mindset} + \text{Support Systems} \qquad (58)$$

This equation reflects the foundation of resilience that Apex built, showing that personal growth is intertwined with the support of a cohesive team. As he continued to navigate the complexities of team dynamics, Apex not only solidified his status as a top fragger but also emerged as a beacon of hope and inspiration for aspiring esports athletes.

Facing Betrayal with Resilience and Determination

In the high-stakes world of esports, the thrill of competition is often accompanied by the shadow of betrayal. For Anjali Esposito, known in the gaming realm as Apex, the unexpected split from his team was not merely a professional setback; it was a profound personal upheaval. This chapter of his journey encapsulates the essence of resilience and determination, two qualities that would define his subsequent rise.

The Weight of Betrayal

The emotional turmoil that accompanies betrayal can be likened to a complex equation, where the variables of trust, loyalty, and ambition interact in unpredictable ways. The sudden fracture within Apex's team was akin to a sudden drop in a stock market, where the value of camaraderie plummeted, leaving a void that was difficult to fill. The betrayal not only shattered his professional aspirations but also tested the very foundation of his self-worth.

$$B = T + L - A \qquad (59)$$

Where:

- B represents the burden of betrayal,
- T is the trust that was broken,
- L symbolizes the loyalty that was expected, and
- A denotes the ambition that was thwarted.

In this equation, the emotional weight of betrayal is felt most acutely when trust and loyalty are high, and ambition is suddenly curtailed.

Resilience: The Counterbalance

Resilience is the antidote to betrayal's sting. Apex's journey towards reclaiming his position in the esports hierarchy was marked by a series of strategic and psychological maneuvers. Drawing inspiration from the likes of legendary figures in sports and entertainment, he channeled his pain into a fierce determination to rise above the adversity.

- **Mental Fortitude**: Apex engaged in rigorous mental conditioning, employing techniques such as visualization and mindfulness. These practices allowed him to reframe his narrative, viewing the betrayal not as a defeat but as a catalyst for growth.
- **Support Systems**: He sought solace in a supportive network of friends and fellow gamers who understood the unique pressures of the esports environment. This camaraderie became a crucial element in his recovery, reinforcing the idea that success is often a collective journey.
- **Skill Enhancement**: Apex dedicated himself to refining his skills, focusing on the mechanics that made him a formidable entry fragger. This period of intense training was not just about improving gameplay; it was about reclaiming his identity and self-efficacy.

Determination: A Driving Force

Determination, the relentless pursuit of one's goals despite obstacles, became the cornerstone of Apex's response to betrayal. His story is a testament to the idea that setbacks can serve as a springboard for greater achievements.

$$D = G + O - R \qquad (60)$$

Where:

- D is the determination,
- G represents goals that are clearly defined,
- O symbolizes the opportunities that arise from adversity, and
- R denotes the resistance faced during the journey.

In Apex's case, the betrayal opened up new opportunities, pushing him to seek out a fresh start with the team Phoenix Rising, where he would not only redefine his career but also reshape the narrative of his life.

Examples from the Field

The world of competitive gaming is rife with stories of athletes who have faced similar betrayals. Consider the case of a renowned player who was ousted from his team just before a major tournament. Instead of succumbing to despair, he leveraged his skills and joined a rival team, ultimately leading them to victory and reclaiming his status in the esports community. This narrative echoes Apex's journey, highlighting the universal truth that resilience and determination can turn the tide in the face of adversity.

In conclusion, facing betrayal is an inevitable part of any competitive landscape, particularly in the volatile world of esports. However, through resilience and determination, players like Apex can navigate these turbulent waters, emerging stronger and more focused than ever before. This chapter serves not only as a reflection of one man's struggle but as an inspiration for all who dare to dream in the high-octane realm of competitive gaming.

The Road to Redemption

Joining a New Team: Phoenix Rising

In the aftermath of the tumultuous split from his previous team, Anjali Esposito, known in the gaming world as Apex, found himself at a crossroads. The weight of betrayal hung heavy on his shoulders, but within the shadows of despair, a flicker of hope emerged. It was during this challenging period that the opportunity to join a new team, aptly named *Phoenix Rising*, presented itself—a name that resonated deeply with his journey of resilience and rebirth.

A New Beginning

The decision to join Phoenix Rising was not made lightly. Apex had spent countless hours reflecting on his past experiences, analyzing the dynamics of team play, and contemplating what he truly desired in his next venture. The allure of Phoenix Rising lay not only in its promise of competitive success but also in its commitment to fostering a supportive and collaborative environment. The team's ethos was simple yet profound: rise from the ashes, learn from adversity, and emerge stronger than before.

In the world of esports, team dynamics can often dictate the trajectory of a player's career. Apex understood that the synergy among team members could either propel them to greatness or lead to disarray. Thus, he approached this new chapter with an open mind and a willingness to adapt. He was determined to contribute positively to the team's culture while also reclaiming his own identity as a top-tier entry fragger.

Building Trust and Chemistry

Joining Phoenix Rising meant integrating himself into a new roster of players, each with their unique skills and personalities. Apex recognized that building trust was paramount. He initiated team-building exercises, encouraging open communication and camaraderie. This approach not only helped to break the ice but also laid the groundwork for a cohesive unit.

One of the first challenges the team faced was establishing effective communication during gameplay. Apex proposed the implementation of a structured call-out system, where each player would have designated roles and responsibilities. This system was rooted in the theory of *team dynamics*, which emphasizes the importance of clear communication channels in achieving collective goals. By fostering an environment where players felt comfortable expressing their thoughts and strategies, Apex aimed to enhance their in-game performance.

$$\text{Team Performance} = \text{Communication} + \text{Trust} + \text{Skill} \qquad (61)$$

This equation encapsulates the essence of what Apex sought to achieve with Phoenix Rising. By prioritizing communication and trust, he believed that the team's overall skill level would be amplified, leading to improved performance in tournaments.

Overcoming Initial Setbacks

Despite the optimism surrounding Phoenix Rising, the initial phase was fraught with challenges. The team struggled to find its footing in the competitive scene, facing formidable opponents and enduring a series of disappointing losses. Apex, however, remained undeterred. He drew upon his past experiences and the lessons learned from his previous team dynamics.

One notable incident occurred during the *Global Esports Championship*, where Phoenix Rising faced off against the reigning champions. The team entered the match with high hopes but quickly fell behind. Apex, embodying the spirit of a true leader, rallied his teammates during a crucial timeout. He reminded them of their collective potential and the importance of resilience. This moment of inspiration became a turning point, igniting a spark within the team.

The Turning Point

The turning point came during the *Regional Qualifiers*, where Phoenix Rising demonstrated remarkable growth. Apex's contributions as an entry fragger were instrumental in securing key victories. His ability to lead the charge, combined with his strategic insights, allowed the team to capitalize on their opponents' weaknesses.

In one memorable match against *Team Valor*, Apex executed a flawless entry strategy, utilizing smoke grenades and flashbangs to create openings for his teammates. The synergy between him and the support players was palpable, showcasing the effectiveness of their communication and trust.

The culmination of their hard work and determination was evident as Phoenix Rising advanced to the finals of the Regional Qualifiers. The atmosphere was electric, and the stakes were high. Apex, fueled by the support of his teammates and the lessons from his past, felt a renewed sense of purpose.

Apex's Resurgence

As Phoenix Rising continued to gain momentum, Apex's performance soared. He not only reclaimed his status as a top entry fragger but also evolved into a more versatile player, adapting his playstyle to suit the team's needs. This adaptability was crucial in the ever-evolving landscape of esports, where strategies must be fluid and responsive.

Apex's journey with Phoenix Rising exemplified the concept of *adaptive leadership*, where a player must not only excel individually but also elevate the performance of the entire team. His ability to pivot his approach based on the strengths and weaknesses of his teammates became a hallmark of his resurgence.

The Road Ahead

With each passing tournament, Apex and Phoenix Rising solidified their reputation as a formidable force in the esports arena. The team's success was not merely measured by trophies but by the resilience and camaraderie they cultivated along the way. Apex's journey from betrayal to belonging had transformed him into a beacon of hope for aspiring gamers.

As they prepared for the upcoming *World Championship*, Apex reflected on the lessons learned during this chapter of his career. He understood that every setback was an opportunity for growth, and every challenge was a stepping stone toward greatness. The spirit of Phoenix Rising was not just about winning; it was about rising together, embracing the journey, and inspiring others to do the same.

In conclusion, joining Phoenix Rising marked a pivotal moment in Apex's career. It was a testament to the power of resilience, teamwork, and the unwavering belief that even in the darkest of times, one can rise again, stronger and more determined than ever. The story of Apex and Phoenix Rising would go on to inspire a new generation of gamers, reminding them that true greatness is forged in the fires of adversity.

Regaining Confidence and Form

In the tumultuous world of esports, confidence can be as ephemeral as a fleeting shadow, especially for a player like Apex, who had faced the sting of betrayal and the subsequent challenges that followed. The journey to regain confidence and form is often a complex interplay of psychological resilience, strategic recalibration, and physical readiness.

Understanding the Psychological Landscape

The first step in regaining confidence is understanding the psychological landscape that surrounds competitive gaming. According to Bandura's Social Cognitive Theory, self-efficacy plays a crucial role in how players approach challenges. Self-efficacy is defined as an individual's belief in their capability to execute behaviors necessary to produce specific performance attainments. For Apex, rebuilding this self-efficacy was paramount.

$$\text{Self-Efficacy} = \frac{\text{Successes}}{\text{Successes} + \text{Failures}} \qquad (62)$$

Apex had to confront his recent failures and reframe them as learning experiences rather than definitive proof of inadequacy. This cognitive restructuring was essential in shifting his mindset from one of defeat to one of potential triumph.

Setting Achievable Goals

Setting achievable goals is another cornerstone of rebuilding confidence. Apex adopted the SMART criteria—Specific, Measurable, Achievable, Relevant, and Time-bound—when outlining his objectives. For instance, instead of aiming to win a major tournament outright, he focused on improving his individual kill/death ratio over the next month.

$$\text{SMART Goals} = \text{Specific} + \text{Measurable} + \text{Achievable} + \text{Relevant} + \text{Time-bound} \qquad (63)$$

This approach not only made his goals more tangible but also provided a series of small victories that could incrementally restore his confidence.

Revisiting Fundamentals

Regaining form in esports often necessitates a return to fundamentals. Apex revisited the basic mechanics of his gameplay, focusing on crosshair placement, movement, and map awareness. This regression to the basics is akin to an athlete returning to their training roots. He engaged in rigorous practice sessions that emphasized these core skills, employing drills designed to sharpen his reflexes and decision-making processes.

For example, Apex utilized aim training software to enhance his precision. The software provided metrics that allowed him to track his improvement over time, reinforcing his sense of progress.

Building a Supportive Environment

Apex recognized the importance of a supportive environment in his recovery process. He surrounded himself with teammates who believed in his capabilities and encouraged open communication. This camaraderie fostered a sense of belonging and reduced the isolation that often accompanies competitive pressure.

Studies have shown that social support is a significant predictor of resilience in competitive environments. Apex's teammates provided not only tactical feedback but also emotional support, creating a safe space for him to express his vulnerabilities.

Embracing a Growth Mindset

Central to Apex's recovery was the adoption of a growth mindset, a concept popularized by psychologist Carol Dweck. A growth mindset is characterized by the belief that abilities can be developed through dedication and hard work. This perspective allowed Apex to view setbacks as opportunities for growth rather than insurmountable obstacles.

$$\text{Growth Mindset} = \text{Challenges} + \text{Effort} + \text{Learning} \qquad (64)$$

By embracing this mindset, Apex began to see his training sessions not merely as a means to an end but as valuable experiences that contributed to his evolution as a player.

Measuring Progress and Celebrating Small Wins

To maintain motivation, Apex implemented a system for measuring his progress. This included tracking his performance metrics in scrimmages and tournaments, as well as documenting personal milestones, such as improvements in his communication with teammates or his ability to adapt to different game scenarios.

Celebrating these small wins was crucial. Each achieved goal, whether it was a personal best in a scrimmage or a successful strategy executed in a match, contributed to a growing sense of competence and confidence.

Conclusion: The Road Ahead

Regaining confidence and form is not a linear journey; it is often filled with ups and downs. For Apex, the combination of psychological strategies, goal setting, fundamental practice, a supportive team environment, and a growth mindset laid the groundwork for his resurgence. As he continued to refine his skills and rebuild his self-efficacy, Apex began to emerge from the shadows of his past, ready to reclaim his place at the forefront of the competitive gaming world.

In the end, the road to recovery is a testament to the resilience of the human spirit, reminding us all that even in the face of adversity, there lies the potential for greatness.

Overcoming Setbacks and Bouncing Back

In the tumultuous world of esports, setbacks are as inevitable as the rising sun. For Anjali Esposito, known by his gamer tag Apex, the journey back to prominence was fraught with challenges that tested not only his skills as a player but also his mental fortitude. In this section, we delve into the strategies Apex employed to overcome adversity and reclaim his position as a leading entry fragger.

Understanding Setbacks

Setbacks can manifest in various forms—team conflicts, personal crises, or sudden changes in the competitive landscape. For Apex, the unexpected team split from Epsilon Esports was a significant blow. The psychological impact of such an event is often profound, leading to feelings of betrayal and self-doubt. According to psychological theories of resilience, individuals who can reframe setbacks as opportunities for growth are more likely to bounce back effectively [?].

The Road to Recovery

Apex's recovery began with a period of introspection. He utilized the following strategies to navigate his way through the emotional turmoil:

- **Self-Reflection:** Apex took time to analyze his performance and emotional state. Journaling became a therapeutic outlet, allowing him to articulate his feelings and identify areas for improvement.

- **Setting New Goals:** Rather than dwelling on past failures, Apex focused on setting achievable short-term goals. This method aligns with the SMART criteria—Specific, Measurable, Achievable, Relevant, and Time-bound [?]. For instance, he aimed to improve his accuracy by 10% over the next month.

- **Building a Support Network:** Recognizing the importance of community, Apex reached out to fellow gamers and mentors who had experienced similar struggles. This network provided emotional support and practical advice, reinforcing the notion that one is not alone in facing challenges.

Mental Health Considerations

The intersection of mental health and performance in esports cannot be overstated. Apex's journey highlighted the importance of addressing mental wellness as a critical component of recovery. Research indicates that athletes who prioritize mental health are better equipped to handle stress and perform under pressure [?].

Apex sought professional help, engaging with sports psychologists who specialized in performance anxiety and mental resilience. Techniques such as cognitive-behavioral therapy (CBT) helped him reframe negative thoughts and develop coping strategies for high-pressure situations. The application of the following equation, derived from the Cognitive Model, illustrates the relationship between thoughts, feelings, and behaviors:

$$B = f(E + T) \qquad (65)$$

where B is behavior, E is the event, and T is the thoughts about the event. By altering his thought processes, Apex was able to influence his behaviors positively, leading to improved performance.

Re-entering the Competitive Scene

With renewed focus and determination, Apex made the pivotal decision to join a new team, Phoenix Rising. This move was not just a career transition; it symbolized a fresh start. The transition involved:

- **Adapting to New Dynamics:** Joining Phoenix Rising required Apex to adapt to a new team culture and dynamics. He embraced this challenge, understanding that flexibility is crucial in team environments.
- **Demonstrating Leadership:** Apex took on a leadership role within the team, mentoring newer players and sharing insights from his experiences. This not only helped solidify his position but also fostered camaraderie and trust among teammates.
- **Consistent Practice and Improvement:** Apex committed to a rigorous training schedule, focusing on both individual skills and team strategies. The application of deliberate practice, as proposed by Ericsson et al. (1993), was instrumental in honing his abilities.

The Power of Perseverance

Apex's story is a testament to the power of perseverance. Each setback became a stepping stone toward greater achievements. The concept of grit, defined by Duckworth et al. (2007) as passion and perseverance for long-term goals, played a significant role in his comeback. Apex's relentless pursuit of excellence not only led to personal victories but also inspired his teammates and fans alike.

In conclusion, overcoming setbacks is not merely about bouncing back; it is about evolving. Apex transformed his challenges into opportunities for growth, demonstrating that resilience is a key ingredient in the recipe for success in esports. His journey serves as a beacon of hope for aspiring gamers, illustrating that with determination, the path to redemption is not only possible but can also lead to greater heights.

The Struggle with Mental Health

Battling Anxiety and Depression

In the high-octane world of esports, where the stakes are as high as the adrenaline, the mental health of athletes often takes a backseat to performance. For Anjali Esposito, known in the gaming realm as Apex, the journey through anxiety and depression became a significant chapter in his life, one that would shape not only his career but also his understanding of the human condition.

Understanding Anxiety and Depression

Anxiety and depression are not merely fleeting feelings of sadness or worry; they are complex psychological conditions that can have profound effects on an individual's life, particularly in high-pressure environments such as competitive gaming. According to the American Psychological Association, anxiety disorders affect approximately 40 million adults in the United States, making them the most common mental illness. Depression, on the other hand, affects around 17 million adults, often leading to debilitating consequences if left unaddressed.

The relationship between anxiety and performance can be described through the Yerkes-Dodson Law, which posits that there is an optimal level of arousal for peak performance. Too little arousal can lead to underperformance, while too much can result in anxiety and a decline in performance. Mathematically, this can be expressed as:

$$P = f(A)$$

where P is performance and A is arousal level. The challenge for Apex was to find that sweet spot amidst the chaos of competition.

The Weight of Expectations

As Apex rose through the ranks, the weight of expectations began to bear down on him. The pressure to perform at the highest levels, combined with the relentless scrutiny of fans and critics alike, exacerbated his anxiety. Each tournament became a battleground not just against rival teams but against his own mind. The fear of failure loomed large, creating a vicious cycle where anxiety led to self-doubt, which in turn affected his gameplay.

A pivotal moment occurred during a major tournament where Apex, battling both internal and external pressures, found himself unable to focus. The cacophony of the crowd, the flashing lights, and the weight of his own expectations culminated in a panic attack. This incident not only impacted his performance but also marked a turning point in his understanding of mental health.

Seeking Help and Building Resilience

Recognizing the need for change, Apex sought help from mental health professionals. Cognitive Behavioral Therapy (CBT) emerged as a powerful tool in his arsenal. CBT focuses on identifying and challenging negative thought patterns, allowing individuals to develop healthier coping mechanisms. Through therapy, Apex learned to reframe his thoughts, transforming "I must win" into "I will do my best."

Additionally, mindfulness practices became integral to his routine. Techniques such as meditation and deep-breathing exercises helped him manage anxiety in real time. Research has shown that mindfulness can reduce symptoms of anxiety and depression by promoting a state of awareness and acceptance. This aligns with the findings of a study published in the journal *Psychological Science*, which demonstrated that mindfulness meditation can lead to significant reductions in anxiety levels.

Creating a Supportive Network

Apex also understood the importance of a supportive network. He began to open up to his teammates, sharing his struggles and fostering an environment where mental health was prioritized. This vulnerability not only strengthened team bonds but also encouraged others to voice their own challenges. The esports community, often seen as a competitive and cutthroat environment, began to shift towards one that valued mental well-being.

An example of this shift can be seen in the initiatives taken by various esports organizations that now include mental health resources as part of their player support programs. Apex became an advocate for mental health awareness in esports, using his platform to encourage dialogue and reduce the stigma surrounding these issues.

The Road to Recovery

Through this journey, Apex learned that battling anxiety and depression is not a linear path; it is filled with ups and downs. There were days when the shadows of doubt crept back in, but the tools he acquired through therapy and support helped him navigate these challenges. He embraced the idea that mental health is a continuous journey, one that requires ongoing attention and care.

In a poignant moment, Apex reflected on his experiences during a live stream, stating, "It's okay to not be okay. What matters is how we choose to rise from it." This sentiment resonated deeply with his audience, inspiring many to seek help and prioritize their mental health.

Conclusion

The battle against anxiety and depression is a formidable one, especially in the high-stakes world of esports. For Apex, this struggle became a defining aspect of his career, shaping not only his gameplay but also his character. By confronting his mental health challenges head-on, he not only found resilience but also became a beacon of hope for others navigating similar paths. His story serves as a reminder that behind every gamer tag lies a human being with their own struggles, triumphs, and the capacity to inspire change.

The Importance of Mental Wellness in Esports

In the high-octane world of esports, where adrenaline surges and competition is fierce, the mental wellness of athletes often takes a backseat to physical performance and strategic prowess. However, the psychological aspect of gaming is just as crucial, if not more so, for sustained success and overall health. As we delve into the importance of mental wellness in esports, we will explore the theoretical frameworks, common challenges, and real-world examples that illustrate the necessity of prioritizing mental health.

Theoretical Frameworks

Mental wellness in esports can be understood through several psychological theories, including the *Cognitive Behavioral Theory* (CBT) and the *Self-Determination Theory* (SDT).

THE STRUGGLE WITH MENTAL HEALTH

Cognitive Behavioral Theory (CBT) posits that our thoughts, feelings, and behaviors are interconnected. In the context of esports, negative thoughts about performance can lead to anxiety, which in turn can impair decision-making and gameplay. For example, a player who believes they will fail in a tournament may experience heightened anxiety, which could cause them to underperform.

The equation representing this relationship can be simplified as:

$$A = f(T, E) \tag{66}$$

where A is anxiety, T represents thoughts, and E represents environmental factors.

Self-Determination Theory (SDT) emphasizes the role of intrinsic motivation in achieving optimal performance. It suggests that when players feel autonomous, competent, and connected to others, their mental wellness flourishes, leading to better performance outcomes. For instance, a player who enjoys the game for its own sake is likely to perform better than one who feels pressured solely by external rewards.

Common Challenges

Despite the growing awareness of mental health issues in esports, several challenges persist:

- **Stigma:** Many players fear that admitting to mental health struggles will be perceived as weakness, leading to reluctance in seeking help.

- **Burnout:** The intense pressure to perform can lead to burnout, characterized by emotional exhaustion, reduced performance, and a sense of detachment. The esports environment often glorifies overwork, making it difficult for players to take necessary breaks.

- **Isolation:** The nature of competitive gaming can lead to social isolation, as players often spend long hours training or competing, which can exacerbate feelings of loneliness and depression.

Real-World Examples

Several high-profile players have publicly shared their struggles with mental health, highlighting the importance of addressing these issues within the esports community.

Example 1: KuroKy - Kuro "KuroKy" Salehi Takhasomi, a professional Dota 2 player, openly discussed his battles with anxiety and depression. He emphasized the need for mental health resources in the esports scene, advocating for a culture that supports psychological well-being.

Example 2: League of Legends - In the League of Legends community, several players have taken breaks to prioritize their mental health. The famous player "Doublelift" announced a hiatus to focus on his mental wellness, showcasing a shift in perspective within the community regarding the importance of mental health.

Strategies for Improvement

To foster a healthier mental environment in esports, several strategies can be implemented:

- **Mental Health Education:** Teams should provide education on mental health to reduce stigma and encourage players to seek help when needed.
- **Professional Support:** Access to sports psychologists or counselors can help players develop coping strategies and manage stress effectively.
- **Work-Life Balance:** Encouraging a balanced lifestyle that includes breaks, physical activity, and social interactions can mitigate burnout and promote mental well-being.

Conclusion

In conclusion, mental wellness is an integral component of success in esports. By understanding the theoretical frameworks, recognizing common challenges, and learning from real-world examples, the esports community can take significant strides toward fostering a supportive environment. As the industry continues to evolve, prioritizing mental health will not only enhance individual performance but also contribute to the overall growth and sustainability of esports as a whole. In the words of Apex himself, "A strong mind is as vital as a strong aim; both are essential to conquer the battlefield."

Seeking Professional Help and Support

In the high-stakes world of esports, where the pressure to perform can be overwhelming, mental health often takes a backseat to the adrenaline of competition. For Anjali Esposito, known to the world as Apex, the struggle with anxiety and depression was not just a personal battle; it was a silent opponent lurking in the shadows of his illustrious career. This section delves into the importance of seeking professional help and support, highlighting the theories behind mental health in competitive gaming, the prevalent challenges athletes face, and the transformative power of therapeutic interventions.

Understanding Mental Health in Esports

Mental health issues are increasingly recognized as significant factors affecting performance in esports. According to the *World Health Organization*, mental health encompasses emotional, psychological, and social well-being, influencing how individuals think, feel, and act. In the context of competitive gaming, athletes like Apex face unique stressors, including:

- **Intense Competition:** The pressure to consistently perform at peak levels can lead to chronic stress, which is detrimental to mental health.

- **Public Scrutiny:** With fame comes the burden of public expectation; every mistake is magnified, leading to increased anxiety.

- **Isolation:** Despite being part of a team, the nature of gaming can be isolating, contributing to feelings of loneliness and depression.

The *Transactional Model of Stress and Coping* proposed by Lazarus and Folkman (1984) posits that stress arises from the interaction between an individual and their environment. In Apex's case, the constant demands of esports created a scenario where his coping resources were often overwhelmed, necessitating professional intervention.

The Benefits of Professional Help

Recognizing the need for help is the first step toward healing. For Apex, this realization came after a particularly challenging tournament where anxiety clouded his performance. Seeking professional help provided several key benefits:

- **Therapeutic Techniques:** Engaging in cognitive-behavioral therapy (CBT) allowed Apex to identify negative thought patterns and develop healthier coping mechanisms. CBT is effective in treating anxiety and depression by helping individuals reframe their thoughts and behaviors.

- **Support Systems:** Professional therapists often encourage the establishment of a support network. For Apex, reconnecting with teammates and friends fostered a sense of community that was crucial for his mental well-being.

- **Skill Development:** Therapy sessions equipped Apex with skills to manage stress, such as mindfulness and relaxation techniques, which are vital during high-pressure situations.

Real-World Examples

Apex's journey mirrors that of many athletes who have faced mental health challenges. For instance, renowned NBA player Kevin Love has been vocal about his struggles with anxiety and depression, advocating for mental health awareness in sports. Love's openness about seeking help has inspired countless athletes to prioritize their mental health.

Similarly, the esports community has begun to recognize the importance of mental wellness. Organizations like *Mindset Gaming* and *Gamers Outreach* provide resources and support for players facing mental health issues, creating a culture where seeking help is normalized rather than stigmatized.

Creating a Culture of Support

To ensure that athletes like Apex can thrive both on and off the virtual battlefield, it is essential to cultivate a culture that prioritizes mental health. This involves:

- **Education and Awareness:** Teams should implement educational programs that inform players about mental health issues and the importance of seeking help.

- **Access to Resources:** Providing access to mental health professionals, either on-site or virtually, can make it easier for players to seek help when needed.

- **Encouragement of Open Dialogue:** Fostering an environment where players can openly discuss their mental health struggles without fear of judgment is crucial for building trust and resilience within teams.

Conclusion

Apex's experience highlights the significance of seeking professional help and support in the esports realm. By addressing mental health openly and constructively, not only can athletes enhance their performance, but they can also pave the way for a healthier, more sustainable career in the competitive gaming landscape. As the esports industry continues to evolve, prioritizing mental health will be vital in shaping the future of this dynamic field, ensuring that legends like Apex can rise, fall, and rise again—stronger than ever.

Rising from the Ashes

Stepping into the Limelight Once Again

As the sun dipped below the horizon, casting a golden hue over the gaming arena, Apex found himself at the crossroads of his career. The tumultuous journey through betrayal and redemption had sharpened his resolve, and now, with a renewed spirit, he was ready to reclaim his place in the esports pantheon. This chapter of his life was not merely a return; it was a renaissance—a glorious re-emergence into the limelight.

The first step in Apex's resurgence was to redefine his gameplay. After the harrowing experience with his previous team, he understood that his style needed to evolve. *Game theory*, a mathematical framework for analyzing competitive situations, became his ally. By applying the principles of game theory, Apex began to explore new strategies that would not only enhance his performance but also outsmart his opponents. The Nash equilibrium, where no player can benefit from changing their strategy while others remain unchanged, became a focal point in his training sessions.

$$\text{Nash Equilibrium: If } (s_1, s_2, \ldots, s_n) \text{ is a Nash Equilibrium, then } u_i(s_1, s_2, \ldots, s_n) \geq \tag{67}$$

This equation illustrated that Apex needed to find a balance between aggression and caution, ensuring that his plays were not only bold but also strategically sound.

In preparation for his return, Apex immersed himself in rigorous training regimens, often practicing for up to twelve hours a day. He meticulously analyzed past tournaments, identifying mistakes and opportunities for improvement. The importance of *mental conditioning* became evident; thus, he enlisted the help of sports psychologists specializing in esports. They introduced him to techniques such as visualization and mindfulness, which helped him maintain focus and composure under pressure.

For example, during a particularly intense scrimmage, Apex applied visualization techniques to picture himself executing flawless maneuvers. This mental rehearsal allowed him to perform with a confidence that had been absent in his previous season. The results were immediate. His kill-death ratio soared, and his team began to notice a palpable shift in his demeanor—he was no longer just a player; he was a leader.

However, stepping back into the limelight was not without its challenges. The esports community is a double-edged sword, where adoration and criticism coexist in a delicate balance. Apex faced scrutiny from fans and analysts alike, who questioned whether he could recapture his former glory. The weight of expectation bore down on him, manifesting in moments of doubt.

In one particularly heated tournament match against Team Pinnacle, Apex found himself in a precarious situation. With his team down two players and the clock ticking, he was thrust into the spotlight. The pressure was immense, but instead of succumbing to fear, he channeled it into motivation. Drawing from his extensive training, he executed a series of calculated plays, ultimately leading his team to a stunning victory. This moment marked a turning point, solidifying his reputation as a resilient competitor.

$$\text{Victory Probability: } P(V) = \frac{K}{K+O} \tag{68}$$

Where K is the skill level of Apex's team, and O is the skill level of the opposing team. This equation highlights the importance of preparation and skill disparity in achieving success. Apex's resurgence was not just about individual talent; it was about teamwork, strategy, and the relentless pursuit of excellence.

As Apex continued to shine, he began to embrace the role of a mentor within his team. He understood that his experiences, both good and bad, could serve as valuable lessons for the next generation of gamers. The concept of *social learning theory* became prominent in his approach. By sharing his journey, he aimed to inspire young players to navigate the complexities of esports with resilience and integrity.

In a heartfelt interview, Apex stated, "I want to show them that failure is not the end; it's merely a stepping stone. Every setback can lead to a comeback if you're willing to learn and adapt." This philosophy resonated deeply within the esports community, as fans and aspiring players alike rallied behind his message.

In conclusion, stepping into the limelight once again was not merely about reclaiming a title; it was about forging a legacy. Apex's journey was a testament to the power of perseverance, strategy, and the indomitable human spirit. As he stood on the stage, basking in the applause of fans, he realized that this was not just a return—it was a celebration of resilience, a triumph over adversity, and a beacon of hope for all who dared to dream in the world of esports.

Triumphs and Victories with Phoenix Rising

After the tumultuous events that led to the unexpected split from his former team, Anjali Esposito, known in the esports world as Apex, found himself at a crossroads. It was a moment steeped in uncertainty, yet it also marked the dawn of a new chapter. Joining Phoenix Rising was not merely a change of scenery; it was an opportunity to redefine his legacy and reclaim his position at the pinnacle of competitive gaming.

Rebuilding Confidence and Form

Upon joining Phoenix Rising, Apex faced the formidable task of rebuilding his confidence. The shadow of his previous experiences loomed large, but he was determined to transform adversity into strength. This period of introspection and growth was crucial. He immersed himself in rigorous practice routines, focusing on both individual skill enhancement and team dynamics.

The psychological aspect of this journey cannot be overstated. As noted in [?], the mental fortitude required in high-stakes environments is paramount. Apex engaged in various mental conditioning exercises, including visualization techniques and mindfulness practices, to enhance his focus and resilience.

$$C = \frac{F}{A} \qquad (69)$$

Where C is confidence, F represents the player's skill level, and A denotes the anxiety levels. Through dedicated practice and mental exercises, Apex aimed to maximize C, thereby minimizing the impact of A.

Overcoming Setbacks and Bouncing Back

The path to redemption was not devoid of challenges. Early matches with Phoenix Rising revealed inconsistencies in teamwork and communication. Apex quickly recognized that success in esports is not merely about individual prowess but also hinges on the synergy within the team.

To address these issues, he initiated a series of team-building exercises, fostering an environment of trust and collaboration. The implementation of strategies based on Tuckman's stages of group development [?]—forming, storming, norming, and performing—proved essential. By guiding his teammates through these stages, Apex helped cultivate a cohesive unit capable of executing complex strategies under pressure.

For instance, during a crucial match against a rival team, Apex demonstrated his ability to adapt and lead. When the team found itself in a precarious situation, he called for a tactical retreat, allowing them to regroup and reassess. This decision not only salvaged the match but also solidified Apex's role as a leader within Phoenix Rising.

Triumphs in Major Tournaments

The culmination of Apex's efforts with Phoenix Rising became evident during the Intel Championship, where the team faced formidable opponents. Their journey to the finals was a testament to their hard work and dedication. Apex's gameplay was nothing short of spectacular, showcasing his signature entry fragging style that had once made him a household name.

In the finals, Phoenix Rising faced Team Pinnacle, a team known for their aggressive strategies and impeccable coordination. The match was a nail-biter, with each round showcasing the skill and determination of both teams. Apex, channeling the spirit of resilience, led the charge in pivotal moments, securing crucial kills that turned the tide in favor of his team.

The final round was a masterclass in strategy and execution. With the score tied, Apex executed a perfectly timed flanking maneuver, catching the opponents off guard. The crowd erupted as he secured the final kill, leading Phoenix Rising to a resounding victory.

$$W = \sum_{i=1}^{n} P_i \tag{70}$$

Where W represents the total wins, and P_i signifies the points earned in each match. This victory not only added to Apex's individual accolades but also reinforced the team's reputation as a rising powerhouse in the esports arena.

Defying the Odds and Proving Critics Wrong

The triumphs with Phoenix Rising were not merely about trophies; they were about defying the odds and silencing critics who doubted Apex's potential after his tumultuous past. The narrative of a fallen star rising from the ashes resonated deeply within the esports community. Apex became a symbol of resilience, inspiring countless aspiring gamers to pursue their dreams despite setbacks.

In interviews post-victory, Apex emphasized the importance of mental health and support systems within esports, highlighting his journey as a testament to the power of perseverance. His story became a beacon of hope, illustrating that even in the face of adversity, one can rise to greatness.

$$I = R \times T \tag{71}$$

Where I represents the impact, R is the resilience shown, and T denotes the time invested in personal and professional growth. Apex's journey exemplified how resilience, when combined with dedication, can lead to significant impact both on and off the stage.

In conclusion, the triumphs and victories with Phoenix Rising marked a pivotal moment in Apex's career. Through unwavering determination, strategic leadership, and a commitment to personal growth, he not only reclaimed his position as a top entry fragger but also established a legacy that would inspire generations to come. The story of Anjali Esposito, the fierce entry fragger, continues to unfold, leaving an indelible mark on the world of esports.

Defying the Odds and Proving Critics Wrong

In the world of competitive esports, the journey of a player is often fraught with challenges, both on and off the digital battlefield. For Anjali Esposito, known to her legions of fans as Apex, the path to redemption was paved with adversity, skepticism, and the indomitable spirit of a true competitor. This section explores how Apex not only defied the odds but also silenced her critics through sheer determination and skill.

The Weight of Expectations

After the tumultuous split from her previous team, the weight of expectations hung heavily over Apex. Critics were quick to question her abilities, suggesting that her rise to fame was merely a flash in the pan. The equation of public perception can be simplified as:

$$E = \frac{P}{C} \tag{72}$$

where E represents expectations, P is public perception, and C is the credibility of the player. For Apex, the sudden dip in credibility due to the team split led to an increase in expectations from both fans and critics alike. The pressure was palpable, yet it was this very pressure that ignited a fire within her.

The Phoenix Rising: A New Beginning

Joining Phoenix Rising marked a pivotal moment in Apex's career. It was not just a new team; it was a chance to redefine herself. The team's motto, "Rise from the ashes," resonated deeply with her, embodying the resilience she needed to overcome the hurdles ahead. The journey to regain confidence was akin to a mathematical function approaching a limit:

$$f(x) = \lim_{x \to a} \frac{g(x)}{h(x)} \tag{73}$$

where $g(x)$ represents her growing skill set, and $h(x)$ symbolizes the barriers she faced. As she worked diligently, the function of her career began to approach the limit of success, proving that the setbacks were merely stepping stones.

Training and Mental Fortitude

Apex understood that to silence her critics, she needed not only to enhance her gameplay but also to fortify her mental resilience. This dual approach is supported by the theory of psychological resilience, which posits that individuals can develop coping strategies to handle stress and adversity effectively.

One of the key strategies Apex employed was visualization, a technique where athletes mentally rehearse their performance. This can be modeled by the equation:

$$V = P \times R \tag{74}$$

where V is the visualization effectiveness, P is the player's focus, and R is the level of realism in the mental imagery. Apex's commitment to this practice allowed her to approach each match with clarity and confidence, enabling her to perform under pressure.

The Unforgettable Comeback

The defining moment of Apex's resurgence came during the Grand Finals of the Intel Championship. Facing off against some of the most skilled players in the world, she executed a series of plays that would go down in esports history. Her performance was not just a display of skill but a testament to her hard work and resilience.

The impact of her victory can be illustrated through the following equation:

$$I = S \times R \tag{75}$$

where I is the impact of her victory, S represents the skill displayed, and R is the resilience shown throughout her journey. Apex's ability to perform at such a high level while overcoming the odds solidified her place in the esports pantheon.

Silencing the Critics

In the aftermath of her triumphant return, the critics who once doubted her were left with little to say. The narrative had shifted dramatically, and Apex had transformed from a figure of speculation to a symbol of perseverance. Her story became an inspiration for many aspiring gamers, proving that with hard work and determination, it is possible to defy expectations.

In conclusion, Anjali Esposito, through her journey as Apex, exemplified the essence of resilience in esports. By facing her challenges head-on and proving her critics wrong, she not only reclaimed her position as a top-tier player but also inspired a generation of gamers to rise above adversity. The legacy of Apex is one of empowerment, a reminder that even in the face of doubt, greatness can emerge.

The Legend Lives On

The Legend Lives On

The Legend Lives On

In the ever-evolving landscape of esports, where the digital battlegrounds are as fierce as any historical conflict, the legacy of a player can often be measured not just in victories, but in the echoes they leave behind. Anjali Esposito, known to the world as Apex, has transcended the role of a mere competitor; he has become a beacon of inspiration, a cultural icon whose influence reverberates throughout the gaming community.

Establishing a Legacy

Apex's journey is a testament to the power of perseverance and talent. His rise from the humble beginnings of a passionate gamer to a top-tier entry fragger is a narrative that many aspiring esports athletes look to for motivation. The legacy he has established is characterized by several key elements:

- **Inspiring the Next Generation of Entry Fraggers:** Apex's gameplay style, characterized by aggressive tactics and unparalleled precision, has set a benchmark for aspiring entry fraggers. He has not only showcased the importance of skill but has also emphasized the need for strategic thinking and teamwork. Young players often cite Apex as a primary influence in their decision to pursue competitive gaming.

- **Apex's Contributions to Game Development:** Beyond his gameplay, Apex has been vocal about the importance of game mechanics and balance. His insights have led to discussions with developers, advocating for changes that enhance the competitive nature of esports. For instance, during the development of a popular FPS title, Apex's feedback on weapon balance significantly influenced gameplay adjustments, ensuring a fair and competitive environment for all players.

Life Beyond Esports

As Apex's career progressed, he began to explore opportunities beyond the confines of the gaming arena. His ventures into various industries reflect a multifaceted personality that extends beyond being a mere player:

- **Exploring New Ventures and Partnerships:** Apex has collaborated with various brands, leveraging his influence to create partnerships that resonate with his audience. This includes launching a line of gaming peripherals designed for optimal performance, which not only showcases his commitment to quality but also his understanding of gamer needs.

- **Giving Back to the Community:** Apex has initiated several charitable efforts, utilizing his platform to raise awareness and funds for mental health, education, and gaming accessibility. His charity streams have generated significant revenue for various causes, reflecting his belief in the power of community and support. Through these actions, Apex has solidified his role as a leader and role model within the esports community.

The Final Chapter

As Apex reflects on his legendary career, he understands the importance of legacy. The impact of his journey is measured not just in accolades but in the lives he has touched and the community he has helped to foster. His story serves as a reminder that the path to greatness is often fraught with challenges, yet it is the resilience and determination to overcome these obstacles that define true legends.

$$L = \sum_{i=1}^{n}(V_i + I_i + C_i) \tag{76}$$

Where:

- L is the legacy score,
- V_i represents the victories achieved,
- I_i symbolizes the impact made on the community,
- C_i denotes contributions to game development and esports.

In conclusion, Apex's legacy is not merely a collection of achievements; it is a living, breathing entity that continues to inspire and influence the world of esports. As new generations of gamers rise to take their place in the competitive arena, they carry with them the lessons learned from Apex's journey. His story is a reminder that greatness is not solely defined by wins and losses, but by the passion, dedication, and impact one leaves behind.

Establishing a Legacy

Inspiring the Next Generation of Entry Fraggers

In the ever-evolving landscape of esports, the role of the entry fragger stands as a beacon of inspiration for aspiring gamers. Anjali Esposito, known in the gaming realm as Apex, has not only dominated the competitive scene but has also become a mentor and a source of motivation for the next generation of entry fraggers. His journey, marked by tenacity and skill, serves as a roadmap for young players eager to carve their own paths in the world of competitive gaming.

The Role of an Entry Fragger

The entry fragger is the vanguard of any esports team, tasked with the critical responsibility of initiating engagements and securing early eliminations. This role requires a unique blend of mechanical skill, game sense, and psychological fortitude. The entry fragger must not only excel in individual performance but also work cohesively with the team to create opportunities for victory. Apex's approach to this role has set a high standard, showcasing how a player can effectively balance aggression with strategy.

Mentorship and Guidance

Apex has taken it upon himself to mentor aspiring entry fraggers, sharing insights and strategies that have propelled him to the top of the competitive hierarchy. He often emphasizes the importance of practice and the relentless pursuit of improvement. As he once said, "Every frag counts, but the journey to becoming a top fragger is paved with countless hours of dedication and learning." This philosophy resonates with young gamers, encouraging them to embrace the grind and refine their skills.

Moreover, Apex has utilized social media platforms and streaming services to engage with his audience, providing tutorials and live commentary on his gameplay.

This approach not only demystifies the complexities of entry fragging but also fosters a sense of community among aspiring players. By sharing his experiences, Apex creates an environment where young gamers feel empowered to ask questions, seek advice, and share their own journeys.

Overcoming Challenges

The path to becoming a successful entry fragger is fraught with challenges, including intense competition, mental health struggles, and the pressure of public scrutiny. Apex's own experiences with setbacks and adversity serve as powerful lessons for the next generation. He openly discusses his battles with mental health, emphasizing the importance of resilience and seeking help when needed. By addressing these issues candidly, he normalizes conversations around mental wellness in esports, encouraging young players to prioritize their well-being.

In his journey, Apex faced numerous challenges, including team dynamics and personal conflicts. His ability to navigate these turbulent waters showcases the importance of adaptability and teamwork. He often advises young players to cultivate strong communication skills and foster positive relationships within their teams, as these elements are crucial for success in the highly competitive esports environment.

Pioneering New Techniques

Apex's innovative playstyle has not only earned him accolades but has also inspired a new generation of entry fraggers to experiment with their approaches to gameplay. By pioneering new techniques and strategies, he has demonstrated that creativity and adaptability are essential in the fast-paced world of esports. Young players are encouraged to think outside the box, explore unconventional strategies, and develop their unique playstyles.

For instance, Apex's use of unconventional weaponry and unexpected positioning has often caught opponents off guard. This willingness to break the mold inspires aspiring entry fraggers to embrace their individuality and find their own niches within the game. The message is clear: while mastering the fundamentals is crucial, innovation can set a player apart in a sea of competitors.

A Lasting Influence

As Apex continues to establish his legacy, his impact on the next generation of entry fraggers will be felt for years to come. His story serves as a testament to the power of perseverance and passion in the face of adversity. By inspiring young players to push their limits, embrace their identities, and foster a sense of community, Apex is not only shaping the future of competitive gaming but also ensuring that the spirit of esports remains vibrant and inclusive.

In conclusion, the inspiration that Apex provides to the next generation of entry fraggers is multifaceted. Through mentorship, innovative gameplay, and a commitment to mental wellness, he embodies the qualities that aspiring gamers should strive for. As they look up to him, they are reminded that the journey to becoming a top entry fragger is not just about securing frags but also about building a legacy that resonates within the esports community.

Apex's Contributions to Game Development

Apex Esposito, known in the gaming world as Apex, has not only made a name for himself as a formidable entry fragger but has also significantly contributed to the evolution of game development within the esports landscape. His unique perspective as a professional player has allowed him to influence various aspects of game design, mechanics, and community engagement. This section delves into the key contributions made by Apex to game development, highlighting his influence on gameplay mechanics, community feedback loops, and the integration of player-centric design philosophies.

Influencing Game Mechanics

One of the most notable contributions of Apex to game development lies in his input on gameplay mechanics. As an entry fragger, Apex has a profound understanding of the dynamics that govern competitive gameplay. His insights have been instrumental in shaping the design of several popular first-person shooters (FPS), particularly in the realm of weapon balancing and movement mechanics.

For instance, in discussions with game developers during beta testing phases, Apex advocated for the implementation of a more nuanced movement system that rewards skilled players while maintaining accessibility for newcomers. This idea was rooted in the theory of *skill-based progression*, where players are encouraged to improve through practice and mastery of game mechanics. The equation that often represents this relationship can be summarized as:

$$P = f(S, T)$$

where P is player performance, S is skill level, and T is time invested in practice. Apex's contributions helped ensure that games not only catered to seasoned players but also provided a welcoming environment for beginners.

Community Feedback and Iteration

Apex has also been a vocal advocate for the importance of community feedback in the game development process. Recognizing that players are the lifeblood of any game, he has consistently emphasized the need for developers to engage with their player base. This approach aligns with the *feedback loop* theory in game design, where player experiences and suggestions directly influence future updates and iterations.

For example, during the development of a major update for a popular esports title, Apex organized a series of community playtests, gathering feedback from both casual gamers and professional players. The data collected during these sessions was analyzed to identify common pain points and areas for improvement. The iterative process can be illustrated by the following model:

$$D_{new} = D_{old} + \Delta D$$

where D_{new} is the new game design, D_{old} is the existing design, and ΔD represents the changes made based on player feedback. This model not only improved the overall gameplay experience but also fostered a sense of community ownership among players.

Player-Centric Design Philosophy

Apex has championed the concept of *player-centric design*, advocating for game mechanics that prioritize player agency and expression. This philosophy emphasizes the importance of allowing players to make meaningful choices that impact their gameplay experience. Apex's influence can be seen in the development of customizable loadouts, character abilities, and dynamic environments that respond to player actions.

The integration of player-centric design can be encapsulated in the following equation, which reflects the relationship between player choice and engagement:

$$E = g(C, A)$$

where E is player engagement, C is the level of choice available, and A represents the agency players feel in their decisions. By pushing for these elements in game design, Apex has helped create immersive experiences that resonate with players on a deeper level.

Legacy of Innovation

As Apex's career continues to evolve, his contributions to game development have left an indelible mark on the industry. His influence extends beyond individual titles, shaping the broader landscape of competitive gaming. Apex's commitment to collaboration with developers, dedication to community engagement, and advocacy for player-centric design have set a precedent for future esports athletes.

In conclusion, Apex's contributions to game development are a testament to the symbiotic relationship between professional players and the gaming industry. By leveraging his experiences and insights, he has not only enhanced the gameplay experience for millions but has also paved the way for a new generation of game designers who prioritize player feedback and innovative mechanics. As esports continues to grow, the impact of Apex's work will undoubtedly resonate for years to come.

Life Beyond Esports

Exploring New Ventures and Partnerships

In the dynamic world of esports, where the boundaries of competition and collaboration often blur, Anjali Esposito, known in the gaming realm as Apex, has ventured beyond the confines of traditional gaming. The transition from a professional esports athlete to a multifaceted entrepreneur is not merely a career shift; it is a strategic exploration of new ventures and partnerships that can redefine one's legacy.

The Landscape of Opportunities

The esports industry has burgeoned into a multi-billion dollar enterprise, creating a fertile ground for innovation and collaboration. Apex recognized early on that the skills honed in competitive gaming—strategic thinking, teamwork, and adaptability—could be leveraged in various business domains.

Theory of Strategic Partnerships The theory of strategic partnerships suggests that collaboration can lead to mutual benefits that surpass what each entity could achieve independently. According to the Resource-Based View (RBV) of the firm, organizations can gain competitive advantages by pooling resources and capabilities. In the context of esports, this could mean partnering with game developers, tech companies, or even lifestyle brands.

Identifying Potential Partners

Apex's approach to exploring new ventures began with identifying potential partners whose values aligned with his brand. For instance, a partnership with a gaming hardware manufacturer could not only enhance his performance but also provide a platform for co-branded marketing initiatives.

Case Study: Collaboration with Tech Giants One notable example of Apex's strategic partnership is his collaboration with a leading gaming peripheral company. The partnership involved co-developing a line of gaming mice tailored to the needs of competitive players. The equation governing the partnership can be summarized as follows:

$$\text{Value Created} = \text{Innovation} + \text{Market Reach} - \text{Cost}$$

Where: - **Innovation** refers to the unique features developed through collaboration. - **Market Reach** is the combined audience of both Apex and the partner company. - **Cost** encompasses the financial investments made by both parties.

This collaboration not only resulted in a successful product launch but also significantly boosted Apex's visibility in the tech community, reinforcing his brand as a pioneer in esports.

Challenges in New Ventures

Despite the potential for success, exploring new ventures is fraught with challenges. One of the primary issues is the alignment of goals between partners. Misalignment can lead to conflicts, as seen in various partnerships within the esports industry. For instance, a partnership that focuses solely on profit maximization may overlook the importance of community engagement, leading to backlash from fans.

Navigating Conflicts To mitigate such conflicts, Apex employed a framework of open communication and shared objectives. Regular meetings and feedback loops were established to ensure both parties remained aligned. The following equation represents the equilibrium of partnership satisfaction:

$$\text{Partnership Satisfaction} = \frac{\text{Shared Goals} + \text{Effective Communication}}{\text{Conflicts}}$$

Where: - **Shared Goals** reflects the common objectives of the partnership. - **Effective Communication** indicates the quality of interactions between partners. - **Conflicts** represents any disagreements or issues that arise.

Expanding Horizons: Lifestyle and Philanthropy

Apex's ventures extend beyond the gaming sphere into lifestyle branding and philanthropy. His collaboration with a fitness brand aimed at gamers exemplifies this expansion. Recognizing the increasing awareness of health and wellness in the gaming community, Apex partnered to promote physical fitness among gamers.

The Impact of Lifestyle Branding The integration of lifestyle branding into Apex's repertoire serves to enhance his image as a well-rounded individual, rather than just a gamer. This approach not only attracts a broader audience but also fosters a community that values balance and well-being.

Philanthropic Endeavors

In addition to commercial partnerships, Apex has also engaged in philanthropic ventures. Collaborating with charities focused on mental health awareness in gaming, he has used his platform to advocate for mental wellness, thereby addressing a critical issue in the esports community.

The Equation of Impact The impact of Apex's philanthropic efforts can be quantified through the following equation:

$$\text{Social Impact} = \text{Awareness} \times \text{Engagement} - \text{Barriers}$$

Where: - **Awareness** refers to the level of knowledge about mental health issues in gaming. - **Engagement** indicates the active participation of the community in mental health initiatives. - **Barriers** represents any obstacles that hinder participation or awareness.

Through these ventures, Apex has not only diversified his career but has also solidified his role as a cultural icon within the esports landscape.

Conclusion

In conclusion, the exploration of new ventures and partnerships has proven to be a transformative journey for Apex. By strategically aligning with brands and causes that resonate with his values, he has expanded his influence beyond gaming, creating a legacy that inspires future generations. As the esports industry continues to evolve, so too will the opportunities for athletes like Apex, who are willing to embrace change and innovate within their fields.

Giving Back to the Community

The esports community is a vibrant tapestry woven from the threads of competition, camaraderie, and creativity. As athletes like Anjali Esposito, known as Apex, rise to the pinnacle of success, they often find themselves at a crossroads: how to leverage their influence and resources to uplift the very community that supported them. Giving back to the community is not just a noble endeavor; it is a vital aspect of sustaining the ecosystem that nurtures talent and passion.

The Importance of Community Engagement

Engagement with the community serves several purposes. First, it fosters goodwill and strengthens the bond between players and fans. Apex understood this early in his career, recognizing that his success was not solely his own but a shared triumph with those who cheered him on. This notion aligns with the **Social Exchange Theory**, which posits that relationships are built on a cost-benefit analysis where individuals seek to maximize their rewards while minimizing costs. In the context of esports, the rewards of community engagement can manifest as increased loyalty, sponsorship opportunities, and a lasting legacy.

Programs and Initiatives

Apex launched several initiatives aimed at giving back to the community. One notable program was the **Apex Academy,** designed to mentor aspiring gamers. The academy provided resources such as coaching, training sessions, and workshops, allowing young talents to hone their skills under the guidance of seasoned professionals. This initiative was not merely a philanthropic effort; it was a strategic move to cultivate the next generation of players who would eventually contribute to the esports landscape.

$$\text{Success Rate} = \frac{\text{Number of Graduates Who Turned Pro}}{\text{Total Number of Graduates}} \times 100 \quad (77)$$

The success rate of the Apex Academy was a point of pride for Anjali, as it reflected the tangible impact of his contributions. By nurturing talent, he was not only giving back but also ensuring the sustainability of the esports community.

Charity Events and Fundraisers

Apex also participated in various charity events and fundraisers, using his platform to raise awareness and funds for important causes. One such event was the **Gaming for Good** tournament, where proceeds went to mental health organizations. This initiative resonated deeply with Apex, as he had faced his own struggles with mental health throughout his career. By sharing his story and advocating for mental wellness, he helped destigmatize these issues within the gaming community.

$$\text{Funds Raised} = \text{Total Participants} \times \text{Entry Fee} \qquad (78)$$

The funds raised during the Gaming for Good tournament exceeded expectations, illustrating the power of community when united for a common cause. Apex's involvement not only brought attention to mental health but also encouraged other players to engage in similar philanthropic efforts.

Building a Legacy Through Sponsorships

In addition to direct engagement, Apex understood the importance of leveraging sponsorships to give back to the community. By partnering with brands that share a commitment to social responsibility, he was able to amplify his impact. For instance, a collaboration with a leading gaming hardware company resulted in a program that provided high-quality equipment to underprivileged gamers. This initiative addressed the issue of accessibility, ensuring that financial barriers did not hinder aspiring players from pursuing their dreams.

The Ripple Effect

The act of giving back creates a ripple effect within the community. Apex's initiatives inspired fellow gamers to follow suit, leading to a culture of philanthropy within esports. This phenomenon aligns with the **Social Learning Theory**, which emphasizes the role of observation and imitation in learning behaviors. As Apex set an example, other players began to recognize their potential to effect change, leading to a collective effort to support various causes.

Challenges and Considerations

While the desire to give back is commendable, it is not without its challenges. One significant issue is the potential for burnout among players who take on too much responsibility. The pressure to constantly engage with the community can lead to mental fatigue, detracting from performance and personal well-being. Apex navigated this challenge by establishing boundaries and prioritizing self-care, allowing him to contribute meaningfully without sacrificing his mental health.

Additionally, there is the risk of misalignment between personal values and the causes supported. Apex was mindful of this, carefully selecting initiatives that resonated with his beliefs and those of his community. This alignment ensured authenticity in his efforts, fostering trust and respect among fans.

Conclusion

In conclusion, giving back to the community is a multifaceted endeavor that encompasses mentorship, charity, sponsorship, and personal engagement. For athletes like Apex, it is an opportunity to leave a lasting legacy that transcends individual achievements. By uplifting others, they not only enrich the community but also cultivate a supportive environment where future generations can thrive. The journey of giving back is ongoing, and as Apex continues to navigate his career, his commitment to the community remains a cornerstone of his identity—a testament to the power of esports to unite, inspire, and transform lives.

Building a Brand and Personal Branding

In the electrifying world of esports, where the stakes are as high as the adrenaline levels, building a personal brand is not merely an option; it is an imperative. For Anjali Esposito, known in the gaming universe as Apex, the journey of personal branding transcended the conventional boundaries of gaming and seeped into the realms of culture, identity, and influence.

The Essence of Personal Branding

Personal branding can be succinctly defined as the practice of marketing oneself and one's career as a brand. In the context of esports, it involves the strategic management of one's public persona, online presence, and the cultivation of a loyal fanbase. The theory of personal branding rests on several key pillars:

- **Authenticity:** In a world saturated with curated images and personas, authenticity stands out. Apex's journey is marked by his genuine passion for gaming, which resonates with fans and aspiring gamers alike.
- **Consistency:** Building a brand requires a consistent message across all platforms. Apex maintained a steady presence on social media, streaming

platforms, and during tournaments, ensuring that his persona remained recognizable and relatable.

- **Engagement:** Interaction with fans is crucial. Apex leveraged social media to engage with his audience, responding to comments, sharing insights, and creating a sense of community.

Challenges in Personal Branding

Despite the potential rewards, the path to establishing a personal brand is fraught with challenges. Apex faced several hurdles:

- **Public Scrutiny:** As a public figure, Apex was under constant observation. Every move he made was scrutinized, and any misstep could lead to backlash. The pressure to maintain a flawless image often weighed heavily on him.

- **Balancing Personal and Professional Life:** The line between personal and professional life can blur in the esports arena. Apex had to navigate the delicate balance of sharing personal insights while maintaining a professional demeanor.

- **Evolving Trends:** The esports landscape is dynamic, with trends shifting rapidly. Staying relevant required Apex to continuously adapt his branding strategies to align with the changing tastes of his audience.

Strategies for Building a Brand

Apex employed several strategies to build his brand effectively:

1. **Leveraging Social Media:** Apex utilized platforms like Twitter, Instagram, and TikTok to share snippets of his gaming life, personal stories, and behind-the-scenes moments. This not only humanized him but also created a deeper connection with his audience.

2. **Collaborations and Partnerships:** Collaborating with other gamers, brands, and influencers expanded his reach. Apex partnered with gaming companies for sponsorships and merchandise, reinforcing his brand's visibility in the industry.

3. **Content Creation:** Apex ventured into content creation, producing engaging videos, tutorials, and streams that showcased his skills and personality. This diversified his brand and attracted a wider audience.

Case Studies and Examples

To illustrate the impact of personal branding in esports, we can look at several notable examples:

- **Ninja (Tyler Blevins):** Ninja transformed from a professional gamer to a cultural icon by building a brand that transcended gaming. His vibrant personality, strategic collaborations, and engagement with fans catapulted him into mainstream media, exemplifying the power of personal branding.

- **Pokimane (Imane Anys):** As one of the leading female streamers, Pokimane's brand is built on authenticity and community engagement. Her ability to connect with her audience on a personal level while maintaining professionalism has solidified her status in the esports community.

Conclusion

In conclusion, building a brand and personal branding in the esports domain is a multifaceted endeavor that requires a blend of authenticity, consistency, and strategic engagement. For Apex, the journey was not just about becoming a top fragger; it was about creating a legacy that inspired a new generation of gamers. As the esports industry continues to evolve, the importance of personal branding will only amplify, making it essential for aspiring athletes to understand and embrace its intricacies. Apex's story serves as a testament to the power of personal branding in shaping not just a career, but an entire culture within the esports universe.

The Final Chapter

Reflecting on a Legendary Career

As the sun sets on the illustrious career of Anjali Esposito, known to the world as Apex, it is time to delve deep into the reflections of a journey that has not only shaped a remarkable athlete but also transformed the landscape of esports. This chapter serves as a poignant reminder of the trials, triumphs, and tribulations that have defined Apex's legacy, an odyssey marked by passion, resilience, and an unyielding spirit.

Apex's career can be likened to a grand symphony, each tournament a movement that contributes to the overall masterpiece. The early notes were filled with uncertainty and experimentation, as he navigated the intricate world of competitive gaming. His initial forays into the esports arena were fraught with challenges, yet they laid the groundwork for the virtuoso he would become. The theory of deliberate practice, as posited by psychologist Anders Ericsson, emphasizes that mastery is achieved through sustained effort and feedback. Apex embodied this principle, dedicating countless hours to refining his skills, analyzing gameplay, and learning from defeats.

$$P = \frac{E}{T} \tag{79}$$

where P represents performance, E is effort, and T denotes time. This equation underscores the notion that consistent effort over time leads to enhanced performance, a truth that Apex lived by as he honed his craft.

As Apex ascended through the ranks, his signature playstyle began to emerge—a blend of aggression and strategic finesse that would come to define him as one of the fiercest entry fraggers in the game. The concept of flow, introduced by psychologist Mihaly Csikszentmihalyi, encapsulates the state of complete immersion and optimal experience that Apex often found himself in during high-stakes matches. It was in these moments that he transcended the ordinary, executing plays that left spectators and opponents alike in awe.

However, the path to greatness is seldom linear. Apex faced numerous adversities that tested his resolve. The betrayal of teammates and the tumultuous politics of esports could have easily derailed his career. Yet, it was during these dark times that he demonstrated remarkable resilience. The psychological concept of grit, defined by Angela Duckworth as passion and perseverance for long-term goals, became a defining characteristic of Apex's journey. He transformed setbacks into stepping stones, using each challenge as an opportunity for growth.

Reflecting on the Intel Championship, a pivotal moment in Apex's career, we see the culmination of years of hard work. The journey to this prestigious tournament was riddled with obstacles, yet Apex's ability to overcome mental roadblocks and adversity was nothing short of inspiring. His unforgettable victory at the championship not only solidified his status as a top-tier player but also served as a testament to his unwavering dedication.

$$V = \frac{R}{C} \tag{80}$$

where V is victory, R represents resilience, and C denotes challenges faced. This equation illustrates that true victory is achieved through resilience in the face of challenges—a principle Apex exemplified throughout his career.

As Apex transitioned into the Epsilon era, he continued to innovate, pushing the boundaries of team strategy and dynamics. His influence on the global esports scene was profound, as he pioneered new techniques that would shape the meta for years to come. The concept of social learning theory, proposed by Albert Bandura, suggests that individuals learn from observing others. Apex's gameplay inspired a generation of gamers, as they sought to emulate his techniques and strategies, further solidifying his legacy.

The rivalry with Team Pinnacle and the epic clashes with Nemesis became legendary narratives within the esports community. These showdowns not only showcased Apex's skill but also highlighted the intense emotional stakes involved in competitive gaming. The psychological toll of high-pressure matches can lead to anxiety and performance issues, yet Apex consistently rose to the occasion, embodying the essence of a true champion.

As we reflect on Apex's journey, it is crucial to acknowledge the impact of mental health in esports. The struggles he faced with anxiety and depression were not merely personal battles but reflections of a broader issue within the gaming community. Apex's willingness to seek help and advocate for mental wellness resonated with fans and fellow players alike, fostering a culture of openness and support.

In the twilight of his career, Apex stands as a cultural icon, a beacon of inspiration for aspiring gamers. His contributions to game development and the esports industry are immeasurable, as he continues to shape the future of competitive gaming. The legacy he leaves behind is not merely one of victories and accolades but of resilience, innovation, and an unwavering commitment to the craft.

Ultimately, reflecting on a legendary career is not just about the accolades and achievements but also about the journey—the friendships forged, the lessons learned, and the indelible mark left on the hearts of fans and fellow gamers. Apex's story is a testament to the power of passion, the importance of mental health, and the transformative nature of esports. As we close this chapter, we are reminded that legends never truly fade; they continue to inspire and ignite the flames of ambition in the hearts of those who dare to dream.

Legacy and Impact on Esports

The legacy of Anjali Esposito, known to the world as Apex, transcends mere statistics and accolades; it is woven into the very fabric of the esports community. Apex's journey is not just a tale of personal triumph but a reflection of the evolution of competitive gaming itself. This section will explore the multifaceted legacy of Apex, examining the profound impact he has had on the esports landscape, the strategies he pioneered, and the cultural significance of his persona.

Redefining Entry Fragging

Apex emerged as a formidable entry fragger, a role traditionally characterized by aggression and risk-taking. However, he redefined this archetype by introducing a calculated approach to fragging, blending instinct with strategy. His playstyle can be encapsulated by the equation:

$$\text{Success}_{\text{Entry Fragger}} = \text{Aggression} + \text{Strategy} + \text{Team Coordination} \quad (81)$$

Where: - $Aggression$ denotes the willingness to engage opponents, - $Strategy$ reflects the tactical decisions made in real-time, - $Team Coordination$ emphasizes the importance of synergy with teammates.

Apex's ability to balance these elements allowed him to not only secure kills but also create opportunities for his team, fundamentally shifting the expectations of what an entry fragger could achieve.

Influence on Game Design

Apex's rise coincided with significant developments in game design, particularly in first-person shooters (FPS). His success prompted developers to consider the dynamics of competitive play more seriously. For instance, the introduction of new mechanics and balance changes in games like *Counter-Strike: Global Offensive* (CS:GO) can be traced back to the demands of professional players like Apex. The equation for game balance can be described as:

$$\text{Game Balance} = \frac{\text{Player Feedback} + \text{Meta Evolution}}{\text{Developer Response}} \quad (82)$$

This relationship highlights how player experiences, such as those of Apex, directly influence game development. His feedback on weapon mechanics, map design, and character abilities has been instrumental in shaping the competitive landscape.

Cultural Icon and Community Engagement

Beyond his gameplay, Apex's persona resonated with fans and aspiring gamers alike. He became a cultural icon, embodying the spirit of resilience and passion that defines esports. His engagement with the community—through streaming, social media, and charity events—set a precedent for how professional gamers interact with their fans. This cultural impact can be represented by the equation:

$$\text{Cultural Impact} = \text{Visibility} \times \text{Engagement} \times \text{Authenticity} \tag{83}$$

Where: - $Visibility$ refers to the presence of the athlete in public forums, - $Engagement$ denotes the interaction with fans and the community, - $Authenticity$ reflects the genuine nature of the athlete's persona.

Apex's authenticity in sharing his struggles and triumphs has inspired countless individuals, encouraging them to pursue their passions in gaming and beyond.

Pioneering New Strategies

Apex's strategic innovations extended beyond individual play. He contributed to the development of team strategies that have become foundational in esports. His emphasis on communication and adaptability within teams introduced a new paradigm in how teams approach matches. The equation for team success can be expressed as:

$$\text{Team Success} = \text{Communication} + \text{Adaptability} + \text{Skill} \tag{84}$$

This equation illustrates that while individual skill remains crucial, the ability to communicate effectively and adapt to changing circumstances is equally vital for success in high-stakes environments.

Lasting Influence on Future Generations

Apex's legacy is perhaps most evident in the way he has inspired the next generation of gamers. His journey from humble beginnings to the pinnacle of esports serves as a beacon of hope and determination. He has become a mentor to many, sharing insights and experiences that encourage young gamers to pursue their dreams. The equation for legacy can be encapsulated as:

$$\text{Legacy} = \text{Inspiration} \times \text{Impact} \times \text{Continuity} \tag{85}$$

Where: - $Inspiration$ reflects the motivation provided to others, - $Impact$ denotes the tangible effects on the industry, - $Continuity$ emphasizes the ongoing influence of his work.

In conclusion, Apex's legacy is a rich tapestry of innovation, cultural significance, and inspirational leadership. His impact on the esports industry is profound, reshaping not only how games are played but also how they are perceived in the broader cultural context. As the esports landscape continues to evolve, the footprints of Apex will undoubtedly guide future generations of players, developers, and fans alike.

Apex's Influence on the Future of Competitive Gaming

The world of competitive gaming has undergone a seismic shift in the last decade, and at the heart of this transformation lies the indomitable figure of Apex. His influence extends far beyond mere statistics and accolades; it resonates through the very fabric of esports culture, shaping the future of competitive gaming in ways that are both profound and enduring.

Innovative Strategies and Playstyles

Apex's signature playstyle, characterized by aggressive entry fragging, has not only set a benchmark for aspiring players but has also influenced team strategies across various titles. His ability to consistently secure early eliminations has led to a paradigm shift in how teams approach engagements. The equation governing his success can be simplified as follows:

$$\text{Success Rate} = \frac{\text{Total Eliminations}}{\text{Total Engagements}} \times 100 \qquad (86)$$

This formula illustrates the importance of early aggression in securing victories. Teams have begun to adopt similar tactics, leading to a more dynamic and fast-paced competitive environment. The rise of aggressive entry fraggers as a critical role in team compositions can be traced back to Apex's influence, as he demonstrated that the ability to initiate fights effectively is paramount to achieving victory.

Mental Resilience and Player Well-Being

Apex's journey has also spotlighted the crucial aspects of mental health and resilience in esports. His candid discussions about battling anxiety and depression have opened up conversations that were once shrouded in stigma. The importance of mental wellness can be encapsulated in the following model:

$$\text{Performance} = f(\text{Skill}, \text{Mental Health}, \text{Team Dynamics}) \qquad (87)$$

In this equation, performance is a function of skill, mental health, and team dynamics. Apex's advocacy for mental health awareness has spurred organizations to prioritize the well-being of their players, leading to the establishment of support systems and mental health resources within teams. This shift not only enhances player performance but also contributes to the longevity of careers in esports.

Cultural Impact and Community Engagement

Apex's rise to prominence has transcended the confines of competitive gaming, positioning him as a cultural icon. His engagement with fans and the broader gaming community has set a precedent for how professional gamers interact with their audiences. By leveraging social media platforms and streaming services, Apex has fostered a sense of community that extends beyond the competition. This engagement can be modeled as follows:

$$\text{Community Engagement} = \text{Content Quality} \times \text{Frequency of Interaction} \quad (88)$$

Here, community engagement is directly proportional to the quality of content produced and the frequency of interactions with fans. Apex's ability to connect with his audience has inspired a new generation of gamers to pursue their passions, thereby expanding the esports ecosystem.

The Evolution of Game Development

Apex's influence is also evident in the realm of game development. His insights into gameplay mechanics and player experiences have been instrumental in shaping the design of competitive titles. Developers are increasingly seeking feedback from professional players to create balanced and engaging gameplay. The relationship can be expressed as:

$$\text{Game Quality} = g(\text{Player Feedback}, \text{Testing}, \text{Community Input}) \quad (89)$$

In this context, game quality is a function of player feedback, rigorous testing, and community input. Apex's involvement in beta testing and feedback sessions has highlighted the importance of player-centric design, ensuring that games are not only competitive but also enjoyable for a wide audience.

Legacy and Future Directions

As we look to the future, Apex's legacy will undoubtedly shape the trajectory of competitive gaming. His role in promoting diversity within esports, advocating for mental health, and influencing game design will serve as a foundation for future generations of players and developers. The future of esports is a tapestry woven from the threads of Apex's influence, where the principles of inclusivity, mental wellness, and innovative gameplay strategies will continue to thrive.

In conclusion, Apex's influence on the future of competitive gaming is multifaceted and profound. From redefining playstyles to advocating for mental health and community engagement, his impact is felt across the entire esports landscape. As the industry continues to evolve, the lessons learned from Apex's journey will guide the next wave of players, teams, and developers towards a brighter and more inclusive future in competitive gaming.

Unauthorized, But Worth It

The Untold Stories and Behind-the-Scenes Moments

In the shimmering world of esports, where the lights dazzle and the stakes soar, lies a tapestry woven with untold stories and moments that define the essence of a champion. Anjali Esposito, known to the world as Apex, navigated through the electrifying highs and crushing lows of competitive gaming, each experience shaping him into the formidable entry fragger he is today. This section peels back the curtain, revealing the behind-the-scenes moments that rarely make it to the spotlight, yet are pivotal in understanding the man behind the gamer tag.

The Early Days: A Glimpse Behind the Curtain

Before the fame, before the accolades, there was a young Anjali, sitting in his dimly lit room, fingers dancing over the keyboard, immersed in a world that felt both like a sanctuary and a battleground. The early days were marked by a series of trials that tested not just his skill, but his resolve.

One particularly poignant moment occurred during a local tournament in Paris, where Apex faced his first major setback. After a series of unfortunate events, including a crucial technical failure and a miscommunication with his teammates, they were eliminated in the first round. The disappointment was palpable, and the weight of expectations pressed heavily on his shoulders. However, it was during this moment of despair that he learned a valuable lesson about resilience.

$$\text{Resilience} = \frac{\text{Overcoming Setbacks}}{\text{Learning from Failure}} \tag{90}$$

This equation became a mantra for Apex, as he embraced the philosophy that every setback was an opportunity for growth.

The Unseen Struggles of Team Dynamics

As Apex climbed the ranks, he quickly discovered that the path to success was littered with challenges, not just from rivals, but within his own team. The dynamics of teamwork in esports can often be as volatile as the games themselves. One particularly tumultuous period was during his time with Epsilon Esports.

Behind the polished façade of victory, tensions simmered. Personalities clashed, egos flared, and the pressure to perform created an environment fraught with anxiety. In one memorable instance, a heated argument erupted between Apex and a teammate over strategy during a critical match. The fallout was significant, leading to a temporary rift that threatened to derail their season.

In the end, it was the open dialogue and willingness to confront their issues that salvaged their team cohesion. Apex learned that communication was not just a tool, but a lifeline in the world of competitive gaming.

The Secrets of the Training Regimen

While fans often see the glamour of tournaments, the reality of an esports athlete's life is a grueling schedule of practice, strategy sessions, and mental conditioning. Apex's training regimen was a well-guarded secret, one that combined physical fitness with cognitive exercises to enhance reaction times and decision-making skills.

Apex often shared a mantra with his teammates:

> "In the game, as in life, the mind is the greatest weapon."

This belief led him to incorporate unconventional practices into his routine, such as meditation and visualization techniques. He would spend hours visualizing himself in-game, executing plays flawlessly, a practice grounded in psychological theories of performance enhancement.

The results were undeniable. Apex's ability to remain calm under pressure became legendary, allowing him to make split-second decisions that often turned the tide of battle in his favor.

The Emotional Toll of Fame

With fame came not only adulation but also an emotional toll that few outsiders could comprehend. The pressure to maintain a public persona while grappling with personal struggles was a delicate balancing act.

One particularly challenging moment came when Apex faced a wave of online criticism following a disappointing tournament performance. The vitriol spewed by keyboard warriors was harsh and unrelenting. In a candid moment shared with his followers during a livestream, he opened up about the impact of such negativity on his mental health.

$$\text{Mental Health} = \frac{\text{Support}}{\text{Criticism}} \qquad (91)$$

This equation served as a reminder that while criticism could be damaging, a strong support network could mitigate its effects. Apex began to prioritize mental wellness, seeking therapy and fostering open conversations about mental health within the esports community.

The Legacy of Untold Stories

As we delve into the untold stories of Apex, it becomes clear that behind every victory lies a myriad of experiences that shaped him. From the early days of struggle to the pressures of fame, each moment contributed to the legend that is Anjali Esposito.

These behind-the-scenes glimpses not only humanize the athlete but also serve as a testament to the resilience of the human spirit. Apex's journey is a reminder that in the world of esports, as in life, the stories that remain untold often hold the most profound lessons.

In conclusion, the untold stories and behind-the-scenes moments of Apex reveal a tapestry rich with emotion, struggle, and triumph. They illustrate that the path to greatness is rarely linear, and that the true essence of a champion lies not just in their victories, but in their ability to rise, learn, and inspire others along the way.

Unfiltered Opinions and Insight from Apex's Inner Circle

In the kaleidoscopic world of esports, where pixels dance like fireflies and adrenaline fuels the heartbeats of players and fans alike, the narrative of Anjali Esposito, known to many as Apex, is as multifaceted as a diamond. To truly appreciate the essence of Apex, one must delve into the voices of those who have walked alongside him—friends, rivals, coaches, and teammates. Their insights, often raw and unfiltered, provide a compelling glimpse into the life of a gaming legend, revealing the man behind the gamer tag.

The Voice of the Teammates

A Bond Forged in Battle   "Playing alongside Apex was like riding a rollercoaster blindfolded," recalls Maxime, a fellow entry fragger who shared the stage with Apex during his rise to fame. "One moment you're soaring high, and the next, you're plummeting into chaos. But that's what made him special—his ability to thrive in the chaos, to find clarity where others saw confusion." This sentiment echoes through the ranks of his former teammates, who often describe Apex as a beacon of energy, capable of igniting the spirits of those around him.

The Unseen Pressure   However, the spotlight isn't without its shadows. "The pressure was immense," reflects Elise, a former coach who witnessed Apex's evolution from a promising player to a cultural icon. "Everyone expected him to perform at an elite level, and while he often delivered, there were moments when the weight of expectations became unbearable." This duality—of being revered yet scrutinized—shaped Apex's journey, creating a complex relationship with fame that many athletes struggle to navigate.

Rivalry and Respect

The Dance of Rivals   "Facing Apex was like dancing with a tempest," admits Jean, the captain of Team Pinnacle, one of Apex's fiercest rivals. "You knew you were in for a fight, but there was always a mutual respect. He pushed me to be better, to think faster." This rivalry, often characterized by fierce competition, also fostered a sense of camaraderie among players. The mutual respect between Apex and his opponents is a testament to the integrity of the esports community, where skill and strategy reign supreme.

Lessons Learned   Jean continues, "Every time we clashed, I learned something new. Apex had this uncanny ability to adapt mid-game, to read the flow and counteract strategies almost instinctively. It's a skill that not many possess." This insight underscores the importance of adaptability in esports, where the landscape can shift in the blink of an eye. Apex's ability to pivot and evolve is a hallmark of his playstyle, a lesson that aspiring gamers can take to heart.

The Role of Coaches and Mentors

Guiding the Flame   "Coaching Apex was like tending to a wildfire," says Marc, a veteran coach who played a pivotal role in shaping Apex's early career. "You had to be careful not to extinguish his spark while also providing the structure he needed to grow." This delicate balance is crucial in the esports realm, where raw talent must be honed into a finely-tuned skill set. Marc emphasizes the importance of mentorship, stating, "It's not just about teaching mechanics; it's about instilling confidence and resilience."

Navigating Mental Health   As the pressures of competition mounted, Marc also became a confidant for Apex, helping him navigate the often-overlooked aspects of mental health in esports. "We talked about anxiety, the fear of failure, and the importance of taking breaks. It's vital for players to understand that their mental well-being is just as important as their in-game performance." This perspective highlights a growing awareness in the esports community regarding the mental health challenges that athletes face.

The Community Perspective

Inspiring the Next Generation   "Apex is more than just a player; he's a role model," states Chloe, a young gamer who idolizes Apex. "He shows us that it's okay to struggle, to face setbacks, and to rise again." This sentiment is echoed by many in the gaming community, who see Apex not only as a competitor but as a source of inspiration. His journey, filled with trials and triumphs, serves as a beacon for aspiring gamers, illustrating the power of perseverance.

The Cultural Impact   The influence of Apex extends beyond the gaming arena. "He's a cultural icon," remarks Leo, a gaming journalist. "His style, his persona, and his gameplay have all contributed to the evolution of esports as a legitimate form of entertainment." This cultural impact is a testament to how one individual can shape perceptions and inspire change within an entire industry.

Conclusion

As we peel back the layers of Apex's story, it becomes evident that the journey of a gaming legend is not solely defined by victories and accolades. It is also shaped by the relationships forged, the lessons learned, and the challenges faced along the way. The unfiltered opinions and insights from Apex's inner circle paint a vivid picture of a player who embodies the spirit of esports—a relentless pursuit of excellence, tempered by humility and resilience.

In the end, the tale of Apex is a reminder that behind every great player lies a network of support, a community of respect, and a legacy that continues to inspire.

As the esports world evolves, so too does the story of Apex, a narrative that is far from over, with new chapters waiting to be written in the annals of competitive gaming.

A Riveting and Unauthorized Biography of a Gaming Legend

In the sprawling universe of esports, where pixels dance and strategies collide, there emerges a narrative so compelling, so rich in texture and depth, that it demands to be told. This is the unauthorized biography of Anjali Esposito, known to the world as Apex—a name that resonates with the fervor of competitive gaming and the spirit of resilience. This biography delves into the untold stories, the raw emotions, and the exhilarating highs and devastating lows that have shaped the legend of Apex.

The Enigma of Apex

From the outset, Apex was more than just a player; he was an enigma wrapped in a gamer tag, a fierce competitor whose journey through the esports landscape was fraught with challenges that would make lesser players falter. The allure of his persona lies not only in his gameplay but in the layers of complexity that define him. To understand Apex is to understand the very essence of competitive gaming—a realm where glory and despair coalesce in an electrifying dance.

Behind the Screens

In the shadows of the limelight, Apex faced adversities that tested the very fabric of his character. The pressures of fame, the expectations from fans, and the relentless pursuit of excellence created a crucible of challenges. The unauthorized nature of this biography allows us to peel back the layers, revealing the man behind the myth. It is here that we confront the reality of mental health struggles, the toll of public scrutiny, and the relentless drive that propelled him forward.

Theoretical Framework: The Psychology of Esports

To comprehend the journey of Apex, we must engage with the theoretical frameworks that underpin competitive gaming. The psychology of esports is a multifaceted domain that encompasses motivation, stress management, and the quest for identity. According to [1], the Self-Determination Theory posits that intrinsic motivation is crucial for sustained engagement in competitive activities. Apex's journey exemplifies this theory; his passion for gaming transcended mere competition, becoming a driving force that fueled his ascent.

$$M = \frac{(I \cdot E) + R}{C} \tag{92}$$

Where:

- M = Motivation
- I = Intrinsic Interest
- E = Effort
- R = Rewards
- C = Challenges

This equation encapsulates the delicate balance Apex navigated throughout his career. The intrinsic interest in gaming combined with unwavering effort led to significant rewards, yet the challenges he faced often threatened to undermine his motivation.

The Trials of Fame

Fame in the esports arena is a double-edged sword. For Apex, the accolades and recognition were hard-won, yet they came with a price. The expectations from fans and sponsors created a pressure cooker environment that could easily lead to burnout. As noted by [2], the phenomenon of 'imposter syndrome' is prevalent among high-achieving individuals in competitive fields. Apex's candid reflections reveal moments of doubt and insecurity, a stark contrast to the confident persona displayed in tournaments.

The Untold Stories

What makes this biography riveting is the collection of untold stories—moments that define not just a player, but a cultural icon. From the late-night gaming sessions filled with laughter and camaraderie to the solitary moments of introspection that followed a crushing defeat, these narratives weave a rich tapestry of experiences. The unauthorized nature of this biography allows for an unfiltered exploration of Apex's life, providing readers with insights that official narratives often gloss over.

Conclusion: A Legend Reborn

As we traverse the landscape of Apex's life, we witness the evolution of a player who transcended the confines of gaming to become a symbol of resilience and determination. The unauthorized biography of Anjali Esposito is not merely a recounting of achievements; it is a celebration of the human spirit in the face of adversity. Apex's story is a testament to the power of passion, the importance of mental health, and the enduring legacy of a gaming legend.

Bibliography

[1] Ryan, R. M., & Deci, E. L. (2000). Self-determination theory and the facilitation of intrinsic motivation, social development, and well-being. *American Psychologist*, 55(1), 68-78.

[2] Krebs, J. (2016). The Psychology of Esports: Understanding the Mental Game. *Journal of Sports Psychology*, 12(3), 45-56.

Index

-doubt, 8, 9, 37, 45, 49, 57, 61, 99

a, 1–22, 24–30, 32–75, 77–100, 102–111, 113–135, 137, 138, 140
ability, 6, 8, 15, 16, 20, 22, 30, 36, 41, 47–50, 53, 57, 60, 61, 71–73, 75, 88, 95, 107, 116, 127, 129–132, 134, 135
acceptance, 77
access, 56
accessibility, 123
achievement, 55
act, 10, 38, 134
acumen, 9, 61
adaptability, 8, 16, 17, 42, 60, 64, 67, 69, 72–74, 86, 92, 116, 130
adaptation, 48, 58–60, 62, 70, 74
addition, 4, 52, 121, 123
admiration, 27
adoption, 95
adoration, 106
adrenaline, 2, 3, 6, 8, 45, 84, 86, 98, 100, 102, 124
adulation, 134
adventure, 1, 2

adversity, 1, 41, 49, 53, 62, 82, 84, 86, 89–91, 93, 95, 96, 107–111, 116, 127, 140
advice, 116
advocacy, 32, 119, 131
advocate, 21, 34, 99, 121, 128
aftermath, 55, 111
age, 3
aggression, 58, 59, 70, 72, 73, 105, 129, 131
agility, 25
aim, 4, 42, 62, 94
air, 54
Albert Bandura, 128
alignment, 120, 124
allure, 56, 91
ambition, 88, 89
amount, 5
analysis, 58
Anders Ericsson, 127
Angela Duckworth, 127
Anjali, 2, 3, 56
Anjali Esposito, 1, 2, 4, 6, 8, 11, 13, 17, 22, 24, 28, 30, 32, 34, 36, 38, 41, 43, 45, 48, 51, 53, 55, 57, 60, 62, 70, 75, 77, 81, 84, 86, 88, 96, 98, 103, 107, 109, 111, 113,

115, 119, 122, 124, 126, 128, 133, 135, 140
Anjali Esposito's, 2
anticipation, 49, 50, 79
antidote, 5, 89
anxiety, 7, 37, 40, 41, 45, 52, 61, 63, 83, 98–100, 103, 128, 134
Apex, 4, 53, 93
apex, 24
approach, 3, 6, 8, 16, 26, 37, 41, 47, 52, 58–60, 64, 66, 68, 70–75, 77, 78, 80, 85–87, 91, 93, 94, 110, 116, 120, 121, 129–131
archetype, 129
arena, 1, 4, 10, 17, 22, 28, 34, 41, 52, 54, 55, 58, 60, 62, 67–70, 82, 86, 93, 114, 115, 126
argument, 85, 134
arousal, 98
art, 69, 75
artist, 19
ascent, 30, 32, 48
aspect, 7, 10, 16, 23, 39, 42, 70, 77, 100, 122
asset, 51
athlete, 1–4, 8, 10, 11, 19, 26–28, 35, 36, 38–40, 85, 94, 119, 126, 134
atmosphere, 3, 5, 12, 46, 50, 53, 58, 67, 68, 84, 85, 87, 92
attack, 12, 99
attention, 13, 18, 34, 66, 70, 100
audacity, 55
audience, 32, 33, 35, 115, 121, 132
authenticity, 22, 29, 33, 37, 38, 124, 126, 130
autonomy, 40
availability, 38

awareness, 16, 17, 21, 56, 94, 99, 101, 121, 131

back, 24, 42, 49, 66, 67, 69, 71, 96, 98, 100, 106, 122, 123, 131, 133, 138
backlash, 27, 120
backseat, 98, 100, 102
badge, 25
balance, 10, 11, 26, 37–39, 41, 58, 59, 61, 63, 66, 105, 106, 121, 129, 139
balancing, 38, 40, 47, 134
banter, 84
basic, 94
battle, 66, 69, 70, 72, 100, 103, 134
battlefield, 24, 67, 86, 104, 109
battleground, 99, 133
beacon, 8, 29, 32, 34, 38, 41, 48, 53, 75, 88, 93, 98, 100, 108, 113, 115, 128, 130
beauty, 67
bedrock, 8
beginning, 1
being, 10, 13, 34, 40, 75, 99, 100, 114, 121, 124, 131
belief, 45, 50, 55, 83, 93, 95, 134
benchmark, 65, 131
benefit, 54
betrayal, 82–85, 88–90, 93, 127
biography, 138, 140
bit, 55
biter, 67, 108
blend, 1, 11, 49, 126
block, 82
blur, 55, 119
bond, 85
box, 17, 48
brand, 29, 33, 120, 121, 124–126

Index

branding, 27, 29, 32, 36, 121, 124, 126
break, 61, 91
breakthrough, 5, 14
breath, 54
breathing, 115
breeding, 7
brilliance, 54, 65
brink, 4, 54
buffer, 29, 51
building, 7, 8, 10, 32, 36, 47, 49, 52, 53, 59, 91, 117, 124, 126
burnout, 36, 62, 123
buzz, 21

cacophony, 54, 99
caliber, 13, 43
camaraderie, 2, 3, 5, 46, 47, 84, 88, 91, 93, 94, 122
capability, 93
capacity, 100
capital, 10
care, 100, 124
career, 1–3, 5, 6, 8, 10, 13, 19, 21, 24, 44–46, 49, 56, 58, 62, 70, 71, 81, 84, 86, 88, 90, 91, 93, 97, 98, 100, 103, 109, 114, 119, 121, 124, 126–128, 139
Carol Dweck, 12, 83, 95
cascade, 36
case, 5, 7, 9, 56, 64, 67, 90
catalyst, 8, 57, 62, 82, 86
caution, 105
celebration, 140
celebrity, 33
center, 40, 86
challenge, 4, 16, 25, 33, 38, 47, 48, 62, 71, 77, 124, 127

champion, 9, 50, 67, 128, 133, 135
championship, 45, 46, 49, 53, 55, 61, 64, 71, 127
chance, 13, 56, 82, 109
change, 8, 26, 33, 34, 59, 60, 82, 100, 107, 122
changer, 40
channel, 12
chaos, 82, 86
chapter, 6, 15, 19, 45, 58, 62, 67, 68, 71, 80, 81, 84, 86, 88, 90, 91, 98, 107, 126
character, 4, 28–30, 64, 80, 100, 129, 138
characteristic, 127
charge, 55, 57, 108
charisma, 33
chasm, 62
chemistry, 57, 58
child, 2
choice, 28, 118
choke, 77
chord, 24
circuit, 68
clarity, 84
clash, 71
class, 32
clattering, 5
clicking, 84
clock, 106
clutch, 2, 14, 67
coaching, 42
cohesion, 42, 57, 58, 134
collaboration, 58, 61, 73, 119–121, 123
collection, 115
combat, 9, 12, 38, 40, 52
combination, 21, 24, 62, 75, 95
commentary, 115

commitment, 3, 4, 10, 22, 32, 42, 48, 60, 65, 84, 91, 109, 117, 119, 123, 128
comms, 73
communication, 14, 47, 53, 58–61, 63, 71–74, 77, 91, 94, 95, 107, 116, 120, 130, 134
community, 2–6, 8, 10–12, 15, 21, 25, 27, 29, 30, 32–36, 38, 41, 42, 44, 55–57, 61, 67, 71, 72, 76, 80, 83, 85, 90, 99, 101, 106, 108, 113, 114, 116–124, 128, 132, 133, 135, 137
company, 120, 123
competence, 95
competition, 2, 4, 6, 7, 10, 11, 21, 24, 29, 39, 46, 57, 62, 65, 67, 69, 71–73, 85, 86, 88, 100, 103, 119, 122, 132
competitiveness, 70
competitor, 4, 50, 53, 72, 106, 109, 113
complacency, 48
complexity, 40
composure, 67
concept, 17, 35, 43, 49, 56, 71, 95, 127, 128
conclusion, 2, 8, 10, 17, 19, 22, 24, 27, 32, 34, 38, 40, 42, 44, 48, 50, 53, 62, 67, 72, 77, 84, 90, 93, 98, 109, 111, 115, 117, 119, 121, 126, 130, 133, 135
condition, 98
conditioning, 134
conduct, 34
confidence, 6, 14, 16, 54, 63, 82, 83, 93–95, 107, 110

conflict, 82, 84, 87, 113
confrontation, 85
confusion, 85
connection, 7, 11, 37
consensus, 87
consistency, 126
console, 84
constant, 6, 37, 59, 62
construction, 33
consumption, 37
contemporary, 32
contender, 13
content, 33, 132
context, 26, 33, 36, 43, 63, 124, 130
contract, 13
contrast, 66
control, 38, 50, 68, 72, 73, 78, 85
controller, 1, 84
cooker, 37
coordination, 73, 77, 108
core, 30, 43, 60, 75, 94
cornerstone, 3, 5, 50, 88
cost, 75
counter, 16, 73, 77
courage, 55
coverage, 21
craft, 14, 22, 128
creation, 42
creativity, 2, 30, 32, 122
crisis, 26
criticism, 5–9, 12, 57, 106, 135
crosshair, 94
crowd, 46, 54, 67, 69, 99, 108
crucible, 17, 22, 45, 49, 56, 138
cry, 25
culmination, 24, 46, 50, 53, 57, 92, 108, 127
cultivation, 6, 22, 124

culture, 13, 32–34, 43, 47, 48, 50, 59, 67, 69, 73, 74, 91, 104, 124, 126, 128, 131
curiosity, 1, 2, 4
curtain, 62, 133
curve, 59, 82
cutthroat, 99
cycle, 37, 63, 99

damage, 85
dance, 38, 88
database, 53
dawn, 60, 107
day, 53
deal, 57
death, 42, 50
decade, 131
decision, 5, 6, 8, 16, 54, 56, 82, 85, 91, 94, 97, 108, 134
decline, 62, 86, 98
decrease, 52
dedication, 3, 4, 13, 14, 24, 32, 34, 49, 57, 62, 83, 95, 108, 115, 119, 127
defeat, 49, 52, 69, 70, 88, 94
deficit, 71
demeanor, 27
depression, 7, 41, 83, 98, 100, 103, 128
depth, 68, 70
design, 35, 117–119, 129, 132
desire, 2, 6, 17, 70, 123
despair, 82, 84, 90, 133
determination, 2, 3, 5, 7, 13, 17, 24, 25, 42, 49, 50, 55, 57, 65, 69, 84, 88–90, 92, 97, 98, 108, 109, 111, 114, 130, 140

development, 17, 22, 35, 41, 72, 84, 86, 117–119, 128–130, 132
dialogue, 36, 41, 77, 100, 134
differentiation, 29
disagreement, 85
disappointment, 133
disarray, 91
discipline, 35, 66
discord, 84
discovery, 2, 6, 11, 38
discussion, 20
display, 67, 110
distraction, 3
diversity, 33, 35, 41, 132
domain, 56, 126
dominance, 60, 62, 66, 70, 71, 84
doubt, 3, 6, 8, 9, 37, 45, 49, 57, 61, 99, 100, 106, 111
down, 71, 86, 99, 106, 110
downfall, 48
dream, 90
drive, 19, 138
drop, 88
dust, 69
dynamic, 26, 27, 30, 34, 69, 70, 72, 74, 77, 119, 131

ebb, 66
ecosystem, 122, 132
edge, 63, 71, 73
effect, 6, 33, 41, 43, 44, 63
effectiveness, 42, 56, 73, 76
efficacy, 29, 93, 95
effort, 127, 139
element, 16
elimination, 54
emergence, 34
emotion, 135

emphasis, 73, 130
empowerment, 111
encounter, 66, 68, 69, 71
encouragement, 2, 4, 9, 10, 50
end, 67, 95, 134, 137
endeavor, 38, 78, 122, 126
enemy, 16, 54, 66, 73, 75, 77
energy, 54, 82
engagement, 10, 22, 27, 33, 35–37, 78, 117–120, 123, 126, 132, 133
enhancement, 8, 50, 107, 134
entertainment, 89
enthusiasm, 5
entity, 115
entrepreneur, 119
entry, 2, 4–6, 14–17, 20, 25, 30, 32, 41, 42, 47–49, 53, 56–58, 60, 66–69, 72–75, 77–81, 85, 91, 92, 96, 108, 109, 113, 115–117, 129, 131, 133
environment, 5, 26, 35, 43, 44, 47, 58, 59, 61, 63, 70, 77, 87, 91, 94, 95, 99, 102, 116, 131, 134
equation, 5, 6, 10, 13–16, 22, 29, 34, 36, 37, 39, 41, 42, 45–48, 58–60, 63, 66, 68, 72, 78, 86, 88, 89, 91, 101, 105, 109, 110, 118, 120, 121, 129–131, 133, 135, 139
equilibrium, 120
equipment, 123
era, 48, 65, 127
essence, 13, 19, 25, 30, 32, 34, 46, 48, 60, 63, 69–71, 86, 88, 91, 111, 128, 133, 135
establishment, 24, 131

ethos, 75, 91
euphoria, 55
event, 5, 45, 48, 53
evolution, 17, 22, 28, 30, 42, 50, 60, 69, 71, 73, 84, 95, 117, 128, 140
example, 16, 26, 27, 30, 32, 42, 50, 61, 72, 73, 77, 94, 99, 118, 120
excellence, 3, 13, 24, 33, 34, 41, 67, 72, 74, 77, 138
exception, 83
excitement, 7, 13, 49, 53
execution, 16, 59, 71, 108
existence, 40
expansion, 121
expectation, 54, 106
experience, 3, 5, 6, 13, 18, 26, 34, 43, 57, 82, 83, 119, 133
experimentation, 126
exploitation, 5
exploration, 2, 119, 121
explorer, 2
exposure, 7
expression, 29
extend, 55, 77, 85, 121
eye, 3

fabric, 69, 128, 131, 138
face, 1, 5, 8, 26, 34, 50, 53, 83, 86, 90, 95, 103, 108, 111, 116, 140
facilitation, 43
factor, 61
failure, 5, 12, 52, 63, 99, 133
fallout, 134
fame, 21, 29, 30, 33, 34, 37, 38, 40, 109, 133–135, 138
family, 1–3, 9, 84

Index 149

fan, 27, 35, 38, 69
fanbase, 26, 33, 35, 37, 124
fandom, 35, 37
fate, 13
fatigue, 124
favor, 54, 69, 108, 134
façade, 134
fear, 5, 12, 16, 63, 79, 99, 106
feedback, 6, 8, 10, 12, 35, 77, 117–120, 127, 129, 132
feeling, 37, 54, 59
fellow, 3, 5, 7, 9, 21, 51, 85, 128
fervor, 4
field, 35, 72, 77
figure, 27, 58, 85, 111, 131
final, 12, 32, 50, 54, 55, 67, 69, 108
finding, 38
fire, 3, 19
fitness, 121, 134
flank, 54, 69
flanking, 61, 108
flash, 109
flashing, 99
flexibility, 47
flourish, 1
flow, 66
fly, 73
focus, 52, 73, 78, 85, 97, 99
footage, 2, 11, 57, 58
footing, 92
force, 32, 60, 62, 68, 93
forefront, 36, 48, 95
foresight, 50, 77
forging, 6
form, 62, 82, 83, 93–95
formation, 26, 28, 66
formula, 36, 46, 53, 68, 131
forth, 49, 67, 69

fortitude, 6, 11, 22, 42, 46, 51, 55, 60–62, 71, 96
fortress, 8
fortune, 54
foster, 27, 102, 114, 116, 117
foundation, 2, 6, 27, 48, 84, 88, 132
fracture, 88
fragger, 2, 4, 6, 14–17, 20, 22, 24, 25, 30, 32, 42, 48, 49, 53, 56, 57, 60, 67, 69, 71, 75, 77, 79–81, 88, 91, 92, 96, 109, 113, 115, 117, 126, 129, 133
fragging, 5, 20, 41, 47, 58, 60, 66, 68, 72–75, 77, 78, 85, 108, 116, 129, 131
fragility, 27
framework, 16, 50, 56, 70, 83, 120
France, 1, 2, 4, 15, 21
frenzy, 67
frequency, 132
friendship, 5
frustration, 49
fuel, 3
fun, 3
function, 110, 131
fundamental, 5, 39, 77, 95
fusion, 32
future, 2, 32, 34, 41, 42, 44, 48, 52, 58, 70, 74, 77, 85, 86, 88, 117, 119, 122, 128, 130–133

gain, 6, 17, 26, 92
gamble, 54
game, 4–6, 9, 11, 14, 17, 18, 22, 35, 40, 44, 50, 54, 55, 57, 60, 61, 65–67, 69–71, 73, 75,

83, 85, 86, 88, 95, 117, 119, 128, 129, 132, 134
gameplay, 2, 4, 5, 8, 9, 11, 12, 20, 21, 25, 29, 32, 33, 36, 41, 42, 48, 53, 55, 57–60, 62, 68, 71–73, 75, 77, 79, 80, 86, 87, 94, 99, 100, 108, 110, 115, 117, 119, 127, 128, 132
gamer, 2, 4, 6, 8, 11, 14, 19, 24, 26, 30, 32, 34, 38, 41, 43, 50, 60, 86, 96, 100, 113, 121, 133
gaming, 1–4, 6, 9–11, 13, 16, 17, 19, 21, 22, 24, 26, 30, 32–37, 41–45, 47, 48, 51, 53, 55, 58, 62, 65, 67–69, 72, 74, 75, 77, 80, 81, 84, 88, 90, 93, 95, 98, 100, 103, 107, 113–115, 117, 119–121, 123, 124, 126, 128, 130–134, 138–140
gap, 21
gathering, 3, 72, 118
gender, 32
generation, 11, 15, 17, 21, 25, 27, 32, 40, 44, 47, 55, 69, 72, 77, 80, 93, 111, 115–117, 119, 126, 128, 130, 132
genesis, 2, 24, 66
genius, 69
glamour, 134
glimpse, 55
globe, 32
glory, 106
goal, 45, 95
greatness, 11, 25, 28, 32, 46, 49, 55, 67, 72, 84, 91, 93, 95, 108, 111, 114, 115, 127, 135

grenade, 77
grit, 127
ground, 7
grounding, 10
groundwork, 2, 44, 58, 60, 91, 95, 127
group, 84
growth, 6, 8, 12, 38, 45, 48, 49, 53, 56, 57, 60, 62, 67, 72, 82, 83, 85, 88, 95, 98, 107, 109, 127, 133
guard, 17, 61, 77, 108
guidance, 4, 9

hallmark, 4, 70
hand, 52, 98
harassment, 7
hardship, 83
hardware, 120, 123
harmony, 86
head, 8, 37, 100, 111
healing, 103
health, 7, 21, 32, 34, 36, 38, 40, 41, 51, 83, 98–104, 108, 121, 124, 128, 131–133, 135, 138, 140
heart, 55, 85, 131
heat, 24
help, 83, 87, 103, 128
Henry Jenkins, 33
hierarchy, 89
high, 6–9, 12, 13, 16, 42, 43, 45, 50, 52, 56, 61, 62, 66, 68, 70, 71, 79, 84–86, 88–90, 92, 98, 100–102, 123, 124, 128, 130
highlight, 21
history, 2, 14, 17, 24, 41, 47, 54, 67–69, 80, 110

Index 151

hobby, 1, 34, 41
honor, 25
hope, 32, 34, 53, 88, 93, 98, 100, 108, 130
hostility, 7
household, 32, 55, 108
hum, 84

ice, 91
icon, 15, 21, 25, 32, 34, 72, 113, 121, 128, 132
idea, 100
identity, 14, 17, 19, 22, 25–29, 32, 38, 50, 70, 72, 82, 86, 88, 91, 124
illness, 98
image, 22, 29, 121
imitation, 44
impact, 6, 7, 15, 21, 27, 29, 32–34, 36, 41, 42, 47, 61, 73, 74, 77, 79, 80, 88, 110, 114–116, 119, 121–123, 126, 128, 130, 133, 135
imperative, 124
implementation, 42, 73
importance, 4, 6, 8, 21, 27, 34, 35, 38, 41, 42, 48, 49, 51, 59, 72, 78, 83, 94, 99–101, 103, 108, 114, 116, 120, 123, 126, 131, 140
improvement, 4, 6, 8, 12, 45, 48, 49, 82, 85, 94, 118
inability, 86
inadequacy, 94
incident, 27, 99
inclusivity, 32, 33, 35, 132
incorporation, 35
increase, 73

individual, 3, 13, 14, 25, 33, 42–44, 46, 49, 53, 56, 58, 61, 68, 72, 80, 93, 98, 107, 119, 121, 130
industry, 4, 26, 34, 36, 59, 71, 119, 120, 122, 126, 128, 130, 133
influence, 21, 30, 32, 34, 35, 42–44, 73, 74, 79, 80, 113, 115, 117, 119, 121, 122, 124, 127, 129, 131–133
influx, 44
information, 72, 73
ingenuity, 75
ingredient, 98
initiative, 59, 123
innovation, 13, 17, 30, 62, 77, 128, 130
insight, 70
inspiration, 4, 8, 24, 29, 30, 34, 62, 85, 87–90, 111, 113, 115, 117, 128
instability, 26
instance, 8–10, 17, 52, 61, 71, 73, 107, 120, 123, 134
instinct, 129
integration, 117, 118, 121
intensity, 69
interaction, 37, 38, 75
interest, 139
interplay, 32, 34, 62, 72, 93
introspection, 85, 107
isolation, 94
issue, 76, 121, 123, 128

joining, 46, 55, 56, 93, 107
journaling, 40
journey, 2–6, 8, 10–15, 17, 19, 22, 24, 28, 30, 32, 34, 38–42,

45, 46, 48, 50, 51, 53, 55,
57, 60–62, 71, 72, 81–83,
86, 88–90, 93, 95, 96, 98,
100, 108–111, 113–117,
121, 124, 126–128, 130,
133
joy, 21
judgment, 63
juxtaposition, 68

key, 48, 50, 58, 61, 76, 87, 98, 103,
110, 113, 117, 124
keyboard, 3, 133, 135
kill, 20, 42, 50, 75, 77, 108
knack, 24
knife, 54
knowledge, 5

labyrinth, 48
lack, 7, 84
landscape, 1, 5–7, 9, 11, 13, 16, 17,
26, 28, 30, 32, 34, 36,
41–43, 48, 58, 59, 62, 67,
68, 70, 72–75, 80, 86, 90,
92, 93, 113, 115, 117, 119,
121, 126, 128–130, 133,
140
launch, 120
layer, 40
lead, 7, 20, 26, 34, 37, 48, 50, 55, 61,
63, 69, 73, 86, 91, 98, 107,
120, 123, 128
leader, 86, 108
leadership, 47, 71, 88, 109, 130
leap, 11
learning, 4, 44, 49, 53, 59, 74, 82, 83,
94, 127, 128
legacy, 15, 17, 19, 22, 28, 32, 34, 42,
44, 55, 67, 70, 71, 74, 77,
80, 107, 109, 111,
113–117, 119, 122, 126,
128, 130, 132, 137, 140
legend, 1, 19, 135, 140
legion, 6, 41
lens, 32, 43, 44, 59, 69, 71, 75
lesson, 52, 133
level, 36, 45, 61, 83, 91, 98
life, 3, 6, 10, 20, 25, 28, 37, 38, 40,
41, 45, 53, 58, 75, 84, 90,
98, 134, 140
lifeblood, 84
lifeline, 134
lifestyle, 121
like, 2, 4, 7, 9, 13, 24, 32, 33, 35, 36,
43, 53, 60, 84, 86, 90, 93,
104, 122, 133
limelight, 60, 83, 106, 138
limit, 110
line, 38, 88, 120
literature, 51, 82
livestream, 135
living, 37, 115
longevity, 131
loop, 10, 35
lore, 69
loss, 27
love, 83
loyalty, 27, 88, 89
Lyon, 2

machine, 50
maestro, 60
magnitude, 22
mainstream, 21
maintenance, 26
making, 5, 6, 8, 16, 26, 56, 94, 98,
126, 134
male, 35, 41

Index

malfunctioning, 84
man, 90, 133, 138
management, 37, 85, 124
maneuver, 54, 61, 69, 77, 108
manner, 59
mantra, 41, 45, 133, 134
manufacturer, 120
map, 68, 69, 72, 78, 94, 129
mark, 4, 34, 67, 71, 109, 119
market, 88
marketability, 27, 29
marketing, 120, 124
masterclass, 108
mastermind, 71
masterpiece, 126
mastery, 52, 73, 127
match, 16, 18–20, 24, 32, 47, 55, 57, 61, 62, 67, 68, 70–72, 77, 84, 95, 106–108, 134
matter, 62
maximization, 120
means, 7, 30, 32, 65, 71, 77, 95
media, 7, 12, 21, 29, 33–35, 37, 40, 69, 115, 132
meditation, 40, 134
meeting, 87
member, 14, 58, 59
mentor, 9, 115, 130
mentorship, 9, 32, 42, 62, 85, 117
merchandise, 29
meta, 8, 11, 73, 79, 80, 128
metaphor, 24
metric, 42
mettle, 45, 70
microscope, 37
middle, 59
milestone, 13
million, 98
mind, 69, 91, 99

mindedness, 47
mindfulness, 21, 40, 52
mindset, 8, 12, 24, 49, 59, 62, 83, 94, 95
misalignment, 124
miscommunication, 133
mix, 13
mobility, 79
model, 21, 32, 35, 41, 64, 79, 118
mold, 29
moment, 1, 3, 5, 13, 14, 19, 24, 41, 45, 46, 49, 52–56, 58, 69, 71, 82, 85, 93, 99, 106, 107, 109, 110, 127, 133, 135
momentum, 6, 54, 77, 92
moniker, 25, 69
morale, 6, 43, 50
motivation, 32, 43, 95, 106, 113, 115, 139
motivator, 3, 30
motto, 109
mouse, 55
move, 7, 97
movement, 15, 94, 126
myriad, 135
myth, 138

nail, 67, 84, 108
name, 2, 17, 24, 25, 32, 55, 108, 117
narrative, 21, 24, 35, 38, 53, 71, 83–85, 90, 108, 111, 113, 138
Nash Equilibrium, 69, 71
nature, 30, 36, 74, 138
necessity, 6, 51, 74, 100
need, 5, 51, 77, 103
negativity, 3, 7, 135
negotiation, 32

Nemesis, 68–71, 128
network, 1, 2, 4, 5, 7–11, 21, 33, 51, 52, 99, 135, 137
news, 85
niche, 30, 34, 41, 44, 72
norming, 84
note, 35
notion, 30, 34
number, 22

objective, 50, 75
observation, 44
occasion, 128
octane, 8, 50, 62, 90, 98, 100
odyssey, 126
offer, 13
on, 1–9, 11, 13, 15, 19, 21, 22, 25, 27, 33, 34, 36, 37, 40, 41, 43, 45, 47, 49, 52–54, 57–59, 61, 62, 66–69, 71, 73, 74, 76–80, 82–87, 91, 93, 94, 98–100, 104, 106, 107, 109, 111, 114–117, 119–121, 123, 124, 126–130, 133, 135
one, 4, 5, 22, 24, 30, 32, 42, 47, 49, 53, 55, 56, 58, 60, 62, 63, 68, 70, 75, 86, 90, 93, 94, 98–100, 106, 108, 111, 115, 119, 124, 128, 134
opening, 3
openness, 34, 41, 58, 128
opinion, 59
opponent, 16, 46, 55, 71, 77, 103
opportunity, 8, 12, 19, 43, 56, 107, 127, 133
optimism, 92
option, 124
orchestra, 54

organization, 13, 47, 58
other, 3, 5, 10, 12, 52, 57, 64, 66, 68, 69, 73, 78, 85, 98
overcoming, 6, 9, 51, 53, 60, 98

pace, 5, 20, 26, 73
pad, 56
pain, 89, 118
pan, 109
panic, 99
paradigm, 72, 130, 131
Paris, 133
part, 3, 13, 37, 47, 51, 52, 83, 85, 90, 99
participation, 3
partnering, 123
partnership, 120
passion, 1–4, 6, 14, 32, 41, 45, 67, 70, 83, 115, 116, 122, 126, 127, 140
past, 52, 53, 58, 91, 92, 95, 108
pastime, 1, 3
path, 1, 3, 6, 11, 13, 21, 22, 32, 38, 48, 62, 98, 100, 107, 109, 114, 125, 127, 134, 135
peak, 21, 23, 98
penchant, 2
perception, 1, 33, 109
performance, 4, 6, 14, 21, 23, 27, 29, 35, 36, 38, 40, 42–44, 47, 49, 50, 52, 57, 59, 61, 63, 67, 72, 80, 91–93, 95, 98–100, 103, 110, 120, 124, 128, 131, 134, 135
performing, 84
period, 5, 48, 62, 84, 86, 87, 107, 134
peripheral, 120

perseverance, 2, 22, 42, 70, 108, 111, 113, 116, 127
person, 11, 17, 39, 84
persona, 25, 28–30, 32, 37, 40, 124, 128, 134
personality, 26, 114
perspective, 41, 52, 69, 87, 95, 117
phase, 46, 49, 84, 92
phenomenon, 21, 32, 33, 41–44, 49, 63, 69, 70
philanthropic, 121
philanthropy, 121
philosophy, 48, 57, 133
pinnacle, 24, 51, 65, 107, 122, 130
pioneer, 120
pitfall, 2
place, 2, 7, 8, 24, 58, 60, 62, 95, 115
placement, 94
plan, 65
planning, 50, 62
platform, 21, 100, 120, 121
play, 3, 5, 22, 43, 44, 47, 63, 68, 69, 71, 73, 91, 130
player, 6, 11, 15, 20, 26, 27, 30, 35, 41, 43, 45, 46, 53–55, 57, 58, 61, 62, 70, 72, 75, 82, 84, 86, 87, 90–93, 95, 96, 99, 109, 111, 113, 114, 117–119, 127, 129, 131, 132, 137, 140
playstyle, 5, 9, 16, 17, 26, 41, 46, 47, 56, 58, 60, 66, 68, 70, 73, 77, 79, 92, 129, 131
plight, 21
point, 3, 46, 48, 54, 57, 77, 85, 86, 99, 106, 122
popularity, 36
position, 62, 89, 96, 107, 109, 111
positioning, 32, 62, 66, 68, 78, 132

post, 108
posture, 75
potential, 4, 12, 16, 42, 50, 56, 58, 69, 73, 94, 95, 108, 120, 123, 125
power, 9, 11, 17, 22, 32–34, 44, 49, 50, 53, 77, 93, 103, 108, 113, 116, 126, 140
powerhouse, 58
practice, 2, 4, 5, 17, 22, 39, 45, 53, 57, 64, 77, 84, 87, 94, 95, 107, 124, 127, 134
precedent, 36, 88, 119, 132
precipice, 2
precision, 25, 54, 70, 94
predator, 24
preparation, 5, 24, 45, 65, 85
presence, 29, 41, 43, 79, 124
present, 52, 59, 62
pressure, 5, 7, 8, 10, 12, 13, 17, 21, 23, 25, 26, 34, 37, 41, 42, 45, 47, 50, 52, 53, 56, 57, 59, 61–63, 65, 67, 71, 83–85, 94, 98, 99, 102, 106, 123, 128, 134
prestige, 48
prevalence, 7
pride, 70, 122
principle, 5, 16, 41, 47, 83, 127
privacy, 40
pro, 11, 12
process, 16, 35, 51, 74, 94, 118
product, 5, 34, 61, 120
profession, 34
professional, 1–4, 6, 10, 11, 13, 27, 34, 38–41, 55, 71, 83, 84, 88, 103, 117–119, 132
professionalism, 12, 35
profile, 101

profit, 120
program, 123
progress, 94, 95
prominence, 35, 41, 44, 61, 96, 132
promise, 91
proof, 94
prospect, 85
prowess, 24, 25, 46, 49, 50, 57, 68, 71, 75, 100, 107
psychologist, 12, 83, 95, 127
psychology, 17, 18, 42, 62, 72
purpose, 82, 92
pursuit, 1–4, 11, 24, 25, 28, 34, 45, 72, 74, 77, 86, 138
push, 17, 19, 43, 67, 77, 117

qualifier, 49, 57
quality, 123, 132
quest, 70
question, 8, 27, 109
quo, 25

race, 32, 73
rate, 73, 122
ratio, 42, 50
razor, 88
re, 24, 59
reach, 24, 55, 62
reaction, 49, 134
readiness, 93
reality, 2, 85, 134, 138
realization, 103
realm, 2, 4, 7, 13, 28, 32, 34, 36, 45, 48, 51, 53, 55, 58, 62, 72, 81, 84, 88, 90, 98, 115, 119, 132
recalibration, 93
recipe, 98
recognition, 4, 6, 14, 21, 22, 73

recounting, 140
recovery, 51, 94, 95
redemption, 84, 98, 107, 109
refinement, 24, 77
reflection, 48, 86, 90, 128
regaining, 93
regimen, 53, 62, 134
regression, 94
reinforcement, 43
relationship, 6, 9, 59, 98, 101, 118, 119, 129, 132
relaxation, 39
relevance, 30
reminder, 19, 34, 41, 54, 55, 100, 111, 114, 115, 126, 135, 137
repertoire, 121
representation, 32–35
reputation, 13, 17, 23, 47, 56, 57, 60, 79, 93, 106
resentment, 84
resilience, 2, 5–7, 9, 14, 21, 25, 30, 32, 38, 42, 46, 47, 49–51, 53, 55, 58, 60–62, 67, 69, 71, 82–86, 88, 90, 93, 95, 98, 100, 108, 110, 111, 114, 126–128, 133, 140
resistance, 60, 76
resolution, 82, 84, 87
resolve, 4, 6, 45, 48, 49, 53, 62, 86, 127, 133
respect, 21, 59, 67, 77, 79, 124, 137
response, 30, 38, 47, 71
responsibility, 33, 34, 123
restraint, 58
restructuring, 52, 85, 94
result, 22, 98
resurgence, 83, 95, 110
retreat, 108

Index 157

return, 10, 83, 94, 111
revelation, 1, 3
review, 57, 59
reward, 16, 68, 85
rhythm, 55
rift, 134
right, 2, 24, 62
rise, 2, 4, 17, 19, 21, 22, 25, 32, 34, 41, 44, 47, 60–62, 72, 88, 89, 91, 93, 108, 109, 111, 113, 115, 122, 131, 132, 135
risk, 16, 54, 56, 66, 68, 78, 85, 124, 129
rival, 16, 57, 59, 70, 73, 79, 90, 99, 107
rivalry, 5, 65–71, 128
road, 2, 3, 8, 11, 12, 19, 48, 53, 84, 95
roadmap, 115
roar, 46
role, 5, 12, 15, 20, 21, 30, 32, 33, 35, 44, 49, 54, 56, 61, 68, 72, 75, 80, 93, 108, 113, 115, 121, 129, 131, 132
rollercoaster, 68, 81
room, 133
roster, 56, 58, 85, 91
round, 16, 54, 69, 108, 133
routine, 40, 52, 134
run, 10
rush, 2, 3, 6, 84, 86

s, 1–10, 19–27, 29, 30, 32–37, 41–43, 46–50, 54–58, 60–80, 84–86, 88–93, 95, 98, 108–110, 113–115, 119–121, 124, 126–134, 140

sadness, 98
saga, 68, 71
sanctuary, 133
satisfaction, 120
scaffolding, 9
scandal, 27
scenario, 16, 37
scene, 2, 7, 10, 11, 22, 25, 30, 35, 41, 47, 48, 59, 60, 62, 73, 77, 79, 92, 115, 127
scenery, 82, 107
schedule, 134
scholarship, 42
score, 66, 108
scoreboard, 19, 57
screen, 1, 41, 53, 55, 84
scrimmage, 95
scrutiny, 21, 23, 29, 37, 47, 56, 57, 85, 99, 106, 138
season, 62, 134
second, 67, 134
secret, 134
section, 32, 43, 58, 60, 96, 103, 109, 117, 128, 133
self, 6–9, 11, 29, 37, 38, 45, 48, 49, 57, 61, 63, 82, 85, 86, 88, 93, 95, 99, 124
sensation, 21
sense, 7, 26, 33, 36, 40, 43, 79, 82, 87, 92, 94, 95, 116, 117, 132
series, 22, 24, 49, 53, 55, 59, 67, 69–71, 73, 83, 89, 92, 94, 106, 110, 118, 133
session, 24, 85
set, 4, 5, 19–21, 34, 36, 41, 42, 47, 56, 60, 64, 65, 68, 73, 77, 80, 86, 88, 119, 131, 132
setback, 2, 84, 88, 133

setting, 2, 4, 5, 20, 38–40, 95
shadow, 88, 93, 107
share, 6, 12, 58, 63, 73, 116, 123
sharing, 36, 37, 40, 99, 116, 130
shift, 8, 26, 30, 34, 35, 44, 59, 72, 78, 84, 99, 119, 131
showdown, 66
side, 68
signature, 5, 9, 16, 17, 60, 66, 108, 131
significance, 25, 128, 130
silence, 84, 110
situation, 54, 84, 85, 106, 107
skepticism, 1, 3, 24, 109
skill, 3–6, 11, 13, 14, 22, 24, 25, 27, 34, 36, 42, 46, 51, 53, 55–57, 61, 62, 67–69, 71, 74, 91, 107–110, 115, 128, 130, 131, 133
skillset, 28
smoke, 77
software, 94
solace, 1, 5
soul, 85
sound, 105
source, 37, 115
space, 41, 75
spark, 4, 30
specialization, 56
spectacle, 41, 68, 71
specter, 49, 62
speculation, 85, 111
sphere, 121
spirit, 1, 24, 30, 50, 53, 67, 71, 72, 83, 95, 108, 109, 117, 126, 140
split, 84–86, 88, 107, 109, 134
sport, 10, 67, 69
sportsmanship, 27

spotlight, 11, 13, 106, 133
squad, 59, 70, 71, 84
stage, 2, 4, 19, 22, 47, 50, 61, 68, 86
standard, 41, 77
standpoint, 41
staple, 73
star, 21, 108
start, 90, 97
status, 14, 25, 32–34, 61, 67, 88, 90, 92, 127
step, 11, 13, 45, 93, 103
stigma, 1, 100
stimulation, 87
sting, 89, 93
stock, 88
stone, 52, 82, 84
storming, 49, 84
story, 2, 15, 21, 24, 27, 30, 35, 41, 42, 53, 62, 67, 93, 100, 108, 109, 111, 114–116, 126, 138, 140
strain, 34
strategy, 3–5, 11, 24, 26, 37, 45, 53, 59, 60, 62, 67, 69, 71–74, 77, 78, 85, 95, 108, 127, 129, 134
streak, 48, 64
streamer, 36
streaming, 21, 35, 38, 115, 132
strength, 1, 47, 107
stress, 10, 21, 40, 42, 51, 110
stretch, 12
string, 84
structure, 72
struggle, 5, 39, 70, 71, 90, 100, 103, 135
student, 4
study, 5, 67
stuff, 47

Index

style, 5, 6, 20, 26, 69, 71, 72, 74, 79, 85, 108
subculture, 32
success, 6, 8, 9, 11–13, 24, 27, 30, 33, 35, 36, 41, 42, 44–48, 50, 53, 57, 60–63, 68, 71, 72, 91, 93, 98, 100, 107, 116, 120, 122, 130, 131, 134
succession, 54
suit, 92
summary, 6, 74, 80
sun, 17, 60, 96, 126
support, 2, 4, 5, 7, 10, 21, 27, 36, 37, 40, 42, 50–52, 83, 88, 92, 99, 100, 103, 108, 128, 131, 135, 137
supremacy, 68, 70–72
surge, 36
surprise, 16, 17, 48
sustainability, 122
sword, 37, 47, 53, 63, 106
symbol, 25, 58, 108, 111, 140
symphony, 54, 60, 126
synergy, 14, 46, 47, 49, 50, 54, 59, 61, 71–74, 77, 91, 107
system, 40, 73, 95

tag, 8, 26, 34, 38, 41, 43, 60, 86, 96, 100, 133
taking, 129
tale, 1, 2, 65, 83, 128, 137
talent, 3, 5, 7, 42, 45, 56, 62, 67, 113, 122
tapestry, 1, 6, 22, 53, 86, 122, 130, 132, 133, 135
target, 7
task, 107
taste, 12

team, 2, 5, 6, 13, 14, 18, 22, 24, 26, 41–44, 46–50, 53–64, 67–75, 77, 78, 82–88, 90–93, 95, 97, 99, 106–109, 116, 127, 129–131, 134
teammate, 82, 85, 134
teamwork, 3, 6, 50, 53, 55, 61, 62, 67, 71, 72, 82, 86, 93, 107, 116, 134
tech, 120
technique, 77, 110
tempest, 8
tempo, 73
tenacity, 115
tendency, 52
tension, 5, 46, 54, 59, 66, 84–86
term, 20, 33, 127
terrain, 7, 17
territory, 16
test, 1, 47, 77
testament, 11, 14, 17, 22, 34, 44, 46, 50, 53, 62, 67, 71, 74, 83, 93, 95, 108, 110, 113, 116, 119, 126, 127, 140
the United States, 98
theorist, 33
theory, 30, 33, 43, 44, 54, 69–71, 75, 110, 124, 127, 128
therapy, 100, 135
thing, 62, 70
thinking, 24, 35, 48
thirst, 1
threat, 62
thrill, 2, 3, 6, 24, 70, 72, 88
thunderstorm, 53
tide, 24, 69, 90, 108, 134
tier, 2, 8, 67, 91, 111, 113, 127
tightrope, 62

time, 10, 18, 21, 26, 38, 39, 41, 53, 55, 94, 126, 134
tipping, 85
title, 17, 24, 46, 73, 118
today, 30, 48, 81, 133
toll, 7, 37, 83, 85, 128, 134, 138
tool, 134
toolbox, 87
top, 2, 8, 11, 14, 17, 22, 24, 40, 47, 60, 62, 67, 71, 88, 91, 92, 109, 111, 113, 117, 126, 127
topic, 20
toughness, 82
tournament, 3, 5, 8, 10, 16, 19, 45, 53, 57, 62, 85, 90, 93, 99, 103, 106, 126, 127, 133, 135
toxicity, 36, 85
trading, 67
training, 12, 42, 53, 54, 56, 62, 94, 95, 106, 134
trajectory, 70, 71, 91, 132
transformation, 28, 50, 86, 131
transition, 4, 11, 13, 46, 55, 58, 82, 97, 119
trepidation, 13
trial, 84
triumph, 34, 42, 46, 48, 53, 55, 57, 71, 84, 94, 128, 135
trust, 47, 59, 71, 82, 86–89, 91, 124
truth, 46, 90
Tuckman, 84
turmoil, 88
turn, 13, 90, 99
turnaround, 83
turning, 3, 46, 54, 57, 86, 99, 106
twilight, 128
twist, 13

uncertainty, 107, 126
underperformance, 98
understanding, 6, 9, 14, 18, 53, 57, 69, 73–75, 78, 93, 98, 99, 133
unison, 54
unit, 49, 91
unity, 50
universe, 124, 126
up, 47, 53, 90, 99, 117, 135
update, 118
upheaval, 88
urgency, 43
use, 17, 50
utilization, 80

validation, 14
value, 6, 38, 88
venture, 91
venue, 53
verticality, 17
viability, 50
victory, 3, 14, 18, 19, 48, 53, 55, 57, 61, 62, 67, 69, 70, 72, 77, 83, 88, 90, 106, 108, 110, 127, 131, 134, 135
view, 8, 82, 95
vigor, 10, 50, 52
virtuoso, 127
visibility, 10, 21, 30, 33, 35, 41, 120
visualization, 52, 110, 134
vitriol, 135
voice, 73, 87, 99
void, 88
vulnerability, 88, 99

wake, 85
warfare, 67, 71, 79
wave, 42, 55, 133, 135

Index

way, 8, 19, 29, 30, 34, 54, 93, 119, 130, 135
wealth, 5
weapon, 73, 129
web, 11, 86
weight, 21, 47, 54, 59, 89, 99, 106, 109, 133
well, 4, 10, 13, 27, 40, 47, 50–52, 58, 65, 77, 95, 99, 121, 124, 131, 134
wellness, 32, 34, 36, 38, 41, 63, 83, 84, 100, 117, 121, 128, 132, 135
whirlwind, 13, 14
willingness, 17, 42, 60, 91, 128, 134
win, 3, 57, 73
winner, 63
winning, 13, 19, 48, 62, 64, 69
won, 55
work, 12–14, 22, 42, 46, 57, 83, 92, 95, 108, 110, 111, 119, 127
workshop, 82
world, 1–4, 6, 8, 11, 13, 15, 17, 19, 22, 24, 27–30, 32, 34, 36, 38, 45, 47, 48, 50, 53, 55, 60–62, 68, 70, 72, 75, 81, 83, 84, 86, 88, 90, 91, 93, 95, 96, 98, 100, 102, 103, 107, 109, 110, 113, 115, 117, 119, 124, 126, 128, 131, 133, 134, 138
worry, 98
worth, 7, 88

year, 4
yoga, 40
youth, 1, 30

zenith, 67
zone, 54

Milton Keynes UK
Ingram Content Group UK Ltd.
UKHW022126051124
450708UK00015B/1200